Going Into The
DEEP
Through
PRAYER

ANNA HAWTHORNE

WESTBOW
PRESS®
A DIVISION OF THOMAS NELSON
& ZONDERVAN

WestBow Press books may be ordered through booksellers or by contacting:

WestBow Press
A Division of Thomas Nelson & Zondervan
1663 Liberty Drive
Bloomington, IN 47403
www.westbowpress.com
844-714-3454

Because of the dynamic nature of the Internet, any web addresses or links contained in this book may have changed since publication and may no longer be valid. The views expressed in this work are solely those of the author and do not necessarily reflect the views of the publisher, and the publisher hereby disclaims any responsibility for them.

Any people depicted in stock imagery provided by Getty Images are models, and such images are being used for illustrative purposes only. Certain stock imagery © Getty Images.

Scripture marked (NKJV) taken from the New King James Version®. Copyright © 1982 by Thomas Nelson. Used by permission. All rights reserved.

Scripture quotations marked (AMP) are taken from the Amplified Bible, Copyright © 1954, 1958, 1962, 1964, 1965, 1987 by The Lockman Foundation. Used by permission.

Scripture quotations marked (ESV) are from the ESV® Bible (The Holy Bible, English Standard Version®), copyright © 2001 by Crossway, a publishing ministry of Good News Publishers. Used by permission. All rights reserved.

Scripture quotations marked (NIV) are taken from the Holy Bible, New International Version®, NIV®. Copyright © 1973, 1978, 1984, 2011 by Biblica, Inc.® Used by permission of Zondervan. All rights reserved worldwide. www.zondervan.com The "NIV" and "New International Version" are trademarks registered in the United States Patent and Trademark Office by Biblica, Inc.®

Scripture quotations marked HCSB are taken from the Holman Christian Standard Bible®, Used by Permission HCSB ©1999,2000,2002,2003,2009 Holman Bible Publishers. Holman Christian Standard Bible®, Holman CSB®, and HCSB® are federally registered trademarks of Holman Bible Publishers.

Scripture marked (KJV) taken from the King James Version of the Bible.

ISBN: 978-1-6642-4168-8 (sc)
ISBN: 978-1-6642-4169-5 (hc)
ISBN: 978-1-6642-4167-1 (e)

Library of Congress Control Number: 2021915254

Print information available on the last page.

WestBow Press rev. date: 08/23/2021

Dedication

I wholeheartedly dedicate this book to God the Father, God the Son, and God the Holy Spirit. Without my Heavenly Father, I can do nothing, but through Jesus Christ I can do all things. I'm grateful to the Holy Spirit for working in me and through me, to accomplish this work.

Dedication

Acknowledgements

First giving all glory to God, who is the Creator of all mankind:

To Angela Nodine, my dear sister-in-Christ, who literally pushed me into doing this project.

To my dear Sisters-in-Christ: Versalle Jones and Angela Nesbitt who dilligently support me in the Sacrificial Prayer Ministry, and encourage me during speaking engagements and other ministries.

To the Sacrificial Prayer Ministry: Without your support, this ministry would not be possible. I am so thankful for each of you.

To my family: You mean the world to me! I am grateful for my children, Alexander and Tonya, and my six beautiful grandchildren; to my mom and step-dad, Helen and Carlton; to my father and step-mom, Ben and Juanita, who always provide Godly, honest counsel; my sisters, Joann and Diana--for their unwavering support and willingness to just 'jump in' when needed; I also must acknowledge my dear friend and sister-in-Christ, Cherylon "Perky" Dean, who has been here from the beginning. We have shared so many wonderful testimonies and life moments together.

To my wonderful husband, Ronnie, who supports me 100% in everything I do. I am abundantly blessed to have him in my life, and I'm eternally grateful to the Father for fullfilling my life with a man who truly loves me for who I am.

It is my prayer that this book not only glorifies God, but blesses every person seeking to go deeper in their prayer life.

Contents

Introduction

GOING INTO THE DEEP THROUGH PRAYER

Welcome! I'm so glad you're here. If you're reading this book, you probably have a desire to go deeper into your prayer life. For most of us, intentional prayer is difficult to maintain; it requires discipline. The great thing about prayer is that it's easy! We can pray anywhere, at any time. Prayer does not require a sophisticated vocabulary, nor a college degree, to go before the Father. However, carving out time for prayer may be very difficult because we are so easily distracted. Prayer often turns into an afterthought, an activity of last resort. We allow the fiery darts of the enemy to knock us down before we pray. We've been granted a privilege that is often ignored, a gift we don't often unwrap until we're desperate.

God's word, from Genesis to Revelations, shows us that prayer unlocks the mysteries of our God. Prayer is how we speak to Him; prayer is how we have communion with the Father; prayer is how we fellowship with Him. So my dear friends, I invite you to join me as we go into the deep through prayer!

This book is a series of eight (8) topics, which can be divided into weekly or monthly sessions, depending on your individual or group goals.

Session 1: *Dynamics of Prayer (Part 1)* – Learn the how, when, why and where to pray.

Session 2: *Dynamics of Prayer (Part 2)* – Discover how key men and women of the Bible gave themselves to prayer and their outcomes.

Session 3: *Praying the Scriptures* – How to use scripture in our prayers.

Session 4: *Meditating Through Scriptures* – How to reflect on the Word of God, and apply it to our lives.

Session 5: *Monologue and Dialogue* - Learn how these styles of prayer are effective.

Session 6: *Pray, Watch, and Wait* – Learn the patience in waiting for God's responses.

Session 7: *Types of Prayer* – Learn about the following prayer types: Adoration, Confession, Consecration, Thanksgiving, Supplication, Intercession, and Worshipping in the Spirit/Tongues.

Session 8: *Trust and Obey*- Explore the importance of trusting God and obeying Him after we have prayed.

Friends, let's begin this journey with a word of prayer:

Father, we thank you in advance for taking us deeper into our prayer life. We present ourselves now as a living sacrifice, holy and acceptable to you. It is our desire to be transformed by the renewing of our minds, and to be fully engaged in prayer. We come with our hearts prepared to unwrap the precious gift you have given us through prayer. We anticipate the signs, miracles and wonders you will perform in and through us. We pray this in the mighty name of our Savior, Jesus Christ.

Amen

Minister Anna Hawthorne

Dynamics of Prayer - Part 1

You may be asking yourself, "How do I pray? When do I pray? Why do I pray?" The answers to these questions are found in the Bible. Sounds simple, right? For some, perhaps; for others, not so much. Before we dive into the dynamics of prayer, I want to begin by telling you a little bit about my personal prayer life.

Before I accepted Christ as my personal Savior, I was introduced to prayer by my grandmother. When I was a little girl, I often spent the night at her house. Before going to bed, my grandmother would lie in bed with me and tell me to say the Lord's Prayer. When I got to the part that says 'deliver us from evil,' Grandma would say, "This is where you pray and ask God for whatever else you need Him to do for you. Then close out the prayer with, for thine is the kingdom, the power, and the glory forever more, Amen."

Friends, this is the way I prayed for a long time, based on how my grandmother instructed me. Did I know Jesus? No. Did I believe in God? Yes, based on what my Grandmother believed in. I know she believed in God, but she could only teach me what she knew; she was never taught about Jesus. Nevertheless, my grandmother's introduction to God planted a seed in me.

Although we did not attend church, I was required to take a weekly Catholicism class in school, and it was boring. In those days, the emphasis was more about Mary, the mother of Jesus, rather than Jesus. I did not learn anything about salvation, but we were taught to pray the rosary, which I still don't understand. All I wanted to do was get through that class with a passing grade.

After leaving home and getting married, I began going to church from time to time. It wasn't until 1994 that I accepted Christ as my Savior. In 1999, the Father began to teach me what prayer was all about. Did He hear my prayers before that time? He absolutely did. You see, God knows every fiber of our being. He prepared me, just as He is preparing you right now. We are all on a journey, and our Father knows just what we need and when we're ready to receive Him. Therefore, let us take a deeper look at prayer.

HOW SHOULD WE PRAY?

The best way to approach prayer is to see how Jesus taught His disciples to pray in Luke 11:1-13. In this chapter, Jesus teaches the disciples what we know as The Lord's Prayer. Clearly, the disciples observed Jesus' prayer life on a daily basis, witnessing how He communed with the Father several times a day. I'm sure their curiosity led them to wanting to know more about prayer. When we are around someone every day and see their lifestyle, it's nearly impossible not to pick up some of their habits, good or bad--which is why we must guard our hearts and watch whom we hang around.

The longer version of the Lord's Prayer, also known as The Model Prayer, is found in Matthew 6:9-13. The difference between the two passages are the context in which they were recorded. In Matthew, the prayer was shared within a large crowd during the Sermon on the Mount. In Luke, Jesus' response was more personal, based on the disciples' question: "how should we pray?" Unfortunately, The Lord's Prayer is usually prayed or recited without much thought to what Jesus says about prayer. Let's look closer at Luke's version of the Lord's Prayer:

1. **When we pray:** Not if, but when we pray. We should be praying on a regular basis. The Father wants our daily attention.

2. **Our Father in heaven:** This makes it personal; we acknowledge He IS our Father.

3. **Hollowed be thy Name:** This means we give the honor that is due to Him; God is holy.

As you can see, true prayer begins by focusing entirely on God. Whether you pray the Model Prayer or if you're praying in your own words, always acknowledge the holiness and sovereignty of God. When we approach the Father, we should do so with humility, honesty and righteousness.

Now, let's look at the next section of the prayer: "Give us day by day our daily bread, and forgive us our sins, for we also forgive everyone who is indebted to us. And do not lead us into temptation, but deliver us from the evil one," Luke 11:3-4 NKJV. The focus now shifts to 'us,' meaning what we need to pray for. In Exodus 16:4, God instructs Moses to tell the children of Israel to gather manna from heaven on a daily basis, just enough for that day. They could have gathered bread for the whole week, but God wanted them to seek His face on a daily basis. God is Jehovah Jireh, our Provider. This passage is our reminder to depend on God. The next verse, "forgive us our sins, for we also forgive everyone who is indebted to us" may be a tough pill to swallow. Does this mean we must ask for forgiveness on a daily basis? Absolutely! We commit sins of omission, failing to do what is right or as instructed, and commission, something we do intentionally. Therefore, we must humbly ask our Father to forgive us.

I John 1:9-10 NKJV tells us: If we confess our sins, He is faithful and just to cleanse us from all unrighteousness. If we say we have not sinned, we make Him a liar, and His word is not in us.

When to Pray

The simple answer to this question should be, ALWAYS! However, we will take a look at what the Word of God says about it. As followers of Christ, it would only be befitting that our prayer life mirrored Jesus. Let's take a look at when Jesus prayed through the scriptures:

Mark1:35 (NKJV): Now in the morning, having risen a long while before daylight, He went out and departed to a solitary place; and there He prayed.

Matt.14:23 (AMP): And after He had dismissed the multitudes, He went up into the hills by Himself to pray. When it was evening, He was still there alone.

Luke 22:44 (NKJV): And being in agony, He prayed more earnestly.

3

Then His sweat became like great drops of blood falling down to the ground.

1 Thessalonians 5:17 (NKJV) Pray without ceasing,

Pretty clear, right? Mark 1:35 states that Jesus prayed early in the morning, before daylight in a solitary place. This further reinforces the importance of making our prayers personal. It's ok to pray with others, but just as Jesus pulled away from the crowds, we also need to find a place of solitude to pray, away from phones, computers, people, etc.

Now let's take a look at Matthew's account. After Jesus left the large crowds, He went into the hills to pray. This passage teaches us that after spending a long day at work, school or even leisure, find a quiet place to talk with the Father. In Luke, we learn about Jesus praying in agony, which reinforces the discipline to pray, even when our spirits are hurting. When we hurt, we often turn to everything outside of Jesus for consolation. Let's not forgot James 5:16: "Therefore confess your sins to each other and pray for each other so that you may be healed. The prayer of a righteous person is powerful and effective." My friends, this passage sums it up. If we want to be like Jesus, we have to pray to Him for guidance, always!

DYNAMICS OF PRAYER PART 1

Study Questions & Devotionals

How Do We Pray? Read Luke 11:1-13

1. What three things should we take note of in the second verse of this passage?

   _____

   _____

   _____

   _____

2. Who does verse two focus on?

   _____

   _____

3. Name three characteristics that should be present when we approach God?

   _____

   _____

4. Who is the focus on in verses 3-4?

   _____

   _____

5. In your own words, why do you think God wanted the Children of Israel to gather bread on a daily basis, instead of once a week?

   _____

   _____

6. What three things did we learn from 1 John 1:9-10?

_____

_____

When Do We Pray? Read Mark 1:35; Matthew 14:23; Luke 22:44, 1 Thessalonians 5:17

1. What are three specific things you learn from Mark 1:35?

_____

_____

2. What does Jesus teach us about the end of the day in Matthew 14:23?

_____

_____

3. How does Jesus' actions compare to ours?

_____

_____

4. What does Luke say about praying in distress?

_____

_____

5. When should we pray?

_____

_____

6. How can I improve my prayer life (your personal goals)?

_____

_____

NOTES:

Devotional

How, When, and Why We Pray

Monday

Psalm 55:16-17 (NKJV): As for me, I will call upon God; And the LORD shall save me. Evening and morning and at noon I will pray, and cry aloud; And He shall hear my voice.

When I wake up in the morning, I call on you, Father, for you are Jehovah Jireh-- you are my provider. When we pray, acknowledge who He is, our King and source of strength. How do we pray? By pouring out our heart to Him. He sits on the throne, waiting for us to come. Regardless of the time of day we pray, we must approach the throne of grace by acknowledging who He is. Jesus constantly communicated with His Father; how much more should we communicate with the all wise, all-knowing God? Morning, noon and night. I will call on your Name. For thine is the kingdom and the power, forever. AMEN

Devotional

How, When, and Why We Pray

Tuesday

Mark 1:35 (NKJV)

Now in the morning, having risen a long while before daylight, He went out and departed to a solitary place; and there He prayed.

Why do you think Jesus rose before daylight to pray? In this context, Jesus is shown as the Son of Man, meaning he is also flesh. He feels what we feel, and His body went through pain just like we do. Just the evening before, Jesus healed sick and demon-possessed people. The entire city gathered in anticipation of Jesus' healing power for their individual lives. Imagine how Jesus felt after healing the throngs of people. Though we cannot compare our lives to Jesus, we can understand how chaotic and draining our lives can be. We normally get up early in the morning; we get the kids ready for school, take care of the house, prepare for work, deal with work-related challenges, pick the kids up from school, prepare dinner (or buy it), attempt to clean house, and help with homework. Whew! When the day is over, we're tapped out and ready for rest. However, after resting our body, what about our soul? We often neglect our inner man. We forget that our soul needs to be refreshed everyday as well. Jesus knew how to go before the Father to renew his Spirit and to gather instructions for the next task. Jesus did this before anyone had the opportunity to request anything of Him. This is WHY we must pray. My dear friends, we need the Father to pour back into us what we have lost. This only happens through prayer.

Right now, stop what you're doing and talk with your Heavenly Father, He's waiting for you.

Devotional

How, When, and Why We Pray

Wednesday

Matthew 14:23 (NKJV): And when He had sent the multitudes away, He went up on the mountain by Himself to pray. Now when evening came, He was alone there.

Jesus sought solitude by going up to the mountain to pray to the Father. We also need to mute our background noise by dedicating some time to spend with Jesus. As mentioned earlier, even Jesus realized the importance of sending the multitudes away. Again, this was not a small group of people—there were 5000 men, not counting women and children! Remember, this is the time when the disciples told Jesus to send the people away. However, Jesus said they could not just send them away without eating. Jesus further instructed them to take a seat, and to feed them. As we often do, the disciples only saw what was in front of them—in this instance, two fish and five loaves of bread---and questioned Jesus' request (Matthew 14:15-23). However, little became much through the power of Jesus.

Now let's take a look at our lives. You ate dinner, the kids are hopefully in bed, the house is tidied up, and you have prepared for the next day. Before going to bed, spend some time in prayer with Jesus and tell Him all about your triumphs and troubles. Let the Father speak to your spirit; let Him renew your strength; let Him prepare you to run and not faint. Turn it over to Jesus, then have a good night's sleep. Wake up refreshed, renewed and ready for a new day.

Devotional

How, When, and Why We Pray

Thursday

Luke 22:44 (NKJV)

And being in agony, He prayed more earnestly. Then His sweat became like great drops of blood falling down to the ground.

If you're on social media, specifically Facebook, you might have heard about 'Thankful Thursday.' As believers, we know every day is a day of Thanksgiving. As you focus on today's scripture, I want you to notice that it says Jesus was in agony. In this context, Jesus' soul was in a state of utmost aguish and grief, to the point of His tears becoming like droplets of blood. Have you ever felt this level of pain before? The disciples, who should have been praying along with Jesus, were sleeping. How many times have you begun to pray, only to fall asleep in the middle of your prayers? Perhaps you are just too overwhelmed with the cares of the world to pray. This is not a coincidence; the enemy will do whatever it takes to keep you from talking to Jesus. Satan is well aware of what happens when you have a made-up mind to pray.

Jesus' soul was grieving because He knew the time had come to be accused by one of His own. He knew that death was near, however Jesus believed the promise of His Father, that in three days He would be raised from the dead. His pain and agony would be temporary, eventually conquering the greatest enemy of all, DEATH. Be encouraged, friends. Know that no matter where you are in life right now, you are not alone. This too shall pass, and you will come out on the other side. Just remember even in your most vulnerable state, PRAY.

Devotional

How, When, and Why We Pray

Friday

1 Thessalonians 5:16-18 (NKJV)

Rejoice always, pray without ceasing, in everything give thanks; for this is the will of God in Christ Jesus for you.

Let's recap this week's lesson. We studied how Jesus taught the disciples to pray through The Lord's prayer. Praying to the father, regardless of the time or circumstance, strengthens our lives. Our text tells us to pray without ceasing, but we should also rejoice in the assurance of knowing that the Father is always listening to our prayers. To pray without ceasing does not mean to literally pray 24/7, but to know that God is always attentive to our prayers. This scripture is often misquoted, with people saying, "How can I give thanks for a bad situation?" In the text, Paul tells us to rejoice in everything, meaning even during tough times, we can be thankful, we can rejoice. No matter how bad the situation is, we have God's promise of eternal life. Hopefully, you can now pray without ceasing.

Dynamics of Prayer - Part 2

The origin of the word *dynamic* comes from the Greek word, *dunamis* which means power. Most of us are familiar with the word dynamite, meaning "energetic", "explosive," and "demonstrative power." Merriam Webster's definition states it is "a pattern or process of change growth, or activity." My definition of dynamic prayer is "prayer that causes change and growth within me that moves me to accomplish God's plan for my life." Through dynamic prayer, God's plan is to prosper us in all we do, by leading and directing our every step. It is through an active prayer life that we will hear His voice.

Another word, similar to power, is authority. In the Greek language, authority or *exousia* is "a right or privilege given to someone by another." In the English language, power and authority are often used interchangeably. For example, does a police officer have the power to stop traffic? A police officer has the *authority* to stop traffic by simply raising their hand. As believers, we have been given authority over Satan in the name of Jesus Christ and by virtue of our testimony. However, we must understand that we do not have power over Satan. There is no way we could stop Satan's devices by ourselves. But through the power of Jesus, we have the authority to trample Satan under our feet. Recognizing the difference between power (dunamis) and authority (excousia) will help us to build a stronger prayer life.

Matthew 6:33 (NKJV): But seek first the kingdom of God and His righteousness, and all these things shall be added to you.

This passage speaks for itself. Before we do anything, we must first seek the kingdom of God, and then everything else will be added. We often look to the world for solutions, totally forgetting the Creator of the world. The Lord's Prayer says "thy will be done." Clearly, the scripture is speaking of God's will; our will must fall in line with God's will, despite what we may want. Take a look at what Hebrews 11 says:

Hebrews 11:6 (NKJV): But without faith *it is* impossible to please *Him,* for he who comes to God must believe that He is, and *that* He is a rewarder of those who diligently seek Him.

In Acts 3:1-8, Peter and John are ministering to a lame man who suffered from this condition since birth. Each day, this man was carried to the city gate, called Beautiful, to beg for money. On this particular day, Peter and John were about to enter the gate when the man called out to them. They instructed the man to pay close attention to what they were about to say. The lame man did as he was told. Peter then said, "Silver and gold I don't have, but I'm willing to give you what I do have. In the name of Jesus Christ of Nazareth, get up and walk." Peter then took the man by the right hand, lifted him up, and immediately his feet and ankle bones received strength. For the first time, this man stood up, jumped and was able to walk with them into the temple.

This passage teaches us several dynamics that need to be present when we pray. Peter and John were on their way to the temple. This man was asking for money, but received more than he could imagine. There are times when we don't know what is best for us, but God does. Peter and John could have just given the man money and gone about their day. Instead, their plans were disrupted. I would venture to say everyone 'stepped out on faith' that day. The miraculous result came from their obedience; the man was made whole. Peter and John used the authority given to them by God through the power Jesus Christ. When they told the man to get up, it wasn't done in their names, but in the name of Jesus. What a great example of faith, obedience, and listening to the Holy Spirit for direction, all ingredients essential for dynamic prayer.

Another example of dynamic prayer comes from Hannah, one of the wives of Elkanah. Hannah could not have children. In those days, a woman unable to bear children, especially a son, was shamed by society. Peninah, Elkanah's other wife, had children. Despite Hannah's condition, Elkanah still loved her, much to the jealousy of Peninah. Consequently, Peninah used every opportunity to remind Hannah of her affliction.

Once a year, the family traveled to Shiloh to present their offering to the Lord. During this time, Hannah was grieved, unable to eat. Elkanah asked why she was upset, saying "am I not better to you than ten sons?" Hannah's grief was out of desperation in wanting a child. After they finished eating and drinking, Hannah desperately prayed to God--with such bitterness and weeping--that Eli, the priest, thought she was drunk. Hannah wasn't drunk, but she appeared to be due to her current situation. Her back was against the wall, so her prayer was laser-focused on the one who could help her, God. Hannah's plea to God was pretty amazing. She stated that if God allowed her to bear a child, she would return it to God! Once Eli realized Hannah was not drunk, he gave her his blessing. The next day, Hannah worshipped God, then returned back to Ramah with her family. Hannah finally conceived, and gave birth to a son whom she named Samuel. Elkanah made another trip to Shiloh to make an offering, but Hannah did not go, deciding to wean Samuel instead. When the time came, Hannah made good on her promise to God, and took Samuel to the temple in Shiloh to Eli. In 1 Samuel, chapter 2, Hannah prays a prayer of Thanksgiving.

Her obedience led to God blessing her with more children. Hannah's life is an example of "laying it all on the altar." We can learn from Hannah by committing ourselves to God, to be obedient to His word, and to activate our faith. Then watch God move on our behalf! Know that God is faithful and just; Scripture says "the prayers of the righteous availeth much." God gives us authority through the power of our Savior, Jesus Christ. Stand firm on His Word, and believe that our Father will answer. He never fails.

DYNAMICS OF PRAYER PART 2

Study Questions & Devotionals

1. Where does the word dynamic originate from?

    _____

    _____

2. Describe the difference between the word power and the word authority?

    _____

    _____

3. As believers, what do we have over Satan?

    _____

    _____

4. In Matthew 6:33, what 2 dynamics do you see in that scripture?

    _____

    _____

5. In the Lord's Prayer, whose will should be done?

    _____

    _____

6. In Hebrews 11:6, what is absolutely necessary when we pray?

    _____

    _____

7. In your own words, why is it impossible to please God without Faith?

    _____

    _____

8. In Hebrews 11:6, what must we believe?

    _____

    _____

9. What happens to those who diligently seek Him?

    _____

    _____

Read Acts 3:1-8

1. What was the lame man asking for? Was he praying?

    _____

    _____

2. Did he receive what he asked for or did he receive God's will?

    _____

    _____

3. How did Peter and John react to the man's request?

    _____

    _____

4. Did they use power or authority to heal this man?

    _____

    _____

Read 1 Samuel Chapters 1-2

1. Why was Hannah in such distress?

    _____

    _____

2. In your own words, how did Hannah react to the criticism she received from Peninnah?

    _____

    _____

3. What was the end result of Hannah's prayer, and how can you incorporate what Hannah did into your own prayer life?

    _____

    _____

4. How did Hannah respond after her prayer was answered?

    _____

    _____

NOTES:

Dynamics of Prayer - Part 2

Monday

Hebrews 11:6 (NKJV) But without faith *it is* impossible to please *Him,* for he who comes to God must believe that He is, and *that* He is a rewarder of those who diligently seek Him.

In the previous section, we discussed Peter and John's interaction, which turned into an interruption, with the lame man at the temple. Has God ever interrupted you on your way to church, work etc.? There are times when God wants us to exercise our faith. Peter and John could have easily kept going, ignoring the man's plea. However, this man was in need of a Savior. We encounter people every day in need of the Savior, but are we willing to stop and exercise the authority given to us by God through Jesus Christ? The deeper we go in prayer, the more our Father will use us in the lives of those in need. When Jesus died for us, he gave us authority to speak in His Name. By His power, the things that are not shall be. Peter and John used the authority given them by Jesus Christ, setting an example for us to do likewise.

Father, I thank you for the authority you have given me through Jesus Christ. Help me to understand and know the difference between power and authority. Please help me to apply these prayer dynamics to use. Give me opportunities to exercise my faith, and to grow daily in my walk with you. In Jesus' name, I will walk in your authority and touch those in need. Use my hands, feet, and my mouth as your earthly representative. May your will be done in my life. I love and adore you Thank you Lord for constantly blessing me, my family, and all who are connected to me.

Amen and Amen.

Dynamics of Prayer -Part 2

Tuesday

In 1 Samuel chapters 1-2, we learned about Hannah, a woman who knew God. Perhaps you have asked God for something, but it seems like He does not hear you. Maybe you made a promise to God, but your prayer still hasn't been answered. For the rest of this week, we will look at how Hannah prayed in her desperate state, after talking and worshipping with the priest. We will see how God answered her prayer and how she responded. Ask yourself "am I in the Fathers will?" Once you have made your request to the Father, give thanks. While you wait, praise and worship Him.

"Heavenly Father, I've made my request known to you. Now as I wait, I thank you because I know that in any situation, you know what's best for me, because Your will is perfect. You are my Lord; I do not lean to my understanding, but trust you completely. For I know that you will direct my path and order my every step. I pray in the precious name of Jesus." Amen.

Dynamics of Prayer - Part 2

Wednesday

1 Samuel 1:13 (NKJV)

Now Hannah spoke in her heart; only her lips moved, but her voice was not heard. Therefore, Eli thought she was drunk.

Today, let's revisit how Hannah prayed in the above scripture. Her heart's desire was to get pregnant. She went to the temple, bowed down before God, but was so grieved by her circumstances that she was unable to utter the words. But in her heart, she was talking with the Father. My dear friends, there will be times when we are so hurt that we cannot speak. Rest assured, our Savior hears all, even our groanings. Eli, on the other hand, assumed she was drunk. Eli, like us, made an assumption about Hannah based on outward appearances. The difference is, God looks at the heart. Our nature is to form an opinion of someone based on what we see. Eli eventually listened to Hannah's predicament and told her to go forth, believing that God would answer her prayer. Prior to Hannah meeting Eli, she was not up to participating in the activities of the feast. However, after speaking with Eli, her appetite and mood returned, which allowed her to worship God before returning home. In a nutshell, Hannah conceived in her spirit that day; she walked away from Eli knowing God heard her prayer. It's important to note that Hannah's joy was evident before the manifestation of the baby's arrival. Friends, if you've been waiting on a prayer to manifest, wipe your tears, straighten up and remember that God can, and will answer prayer. Remember, "faith is the substance of things hoped for and the evidence of things not seen." Believe it is already done. Amen

Dynamics of Prayer - Part 2

Thursday

1 Samuel 1:20 (NKJV)

So it came to pass in the process of time that Hannah conceived and bore a son, and called his name Samuel, *saying,* "Because I have asked for him from the LORD."

Look at the mighty, all-knowing God we serve! In God's time, Hannah's dream was realized; she conceived and bore a son. Not only did God answer her prayer and blessed her with a child, but God gave her exactly what she asked for, a son. Hannah made a vow to God that she would dedicate her child back to God. Hannah began this process by calling her child 'Samuel,' instead of naming him after his father which was customary in that day. Samuel means "asked of God, heard of God." Hannah honored her promise to God. When Samuel was weaned, she took him to the temple and dedicated him to God. Have you ever made a promise to God?

Perhaps you are in a desperate situation right now. Today is the day to give it to the Father because he sees and hears you. He knows your pain, just trust Him. Get up from that place of sorrow, depression, disappointment, or hurt and rise up. Wipe the tears from your eyes and know that God loves you more than anything. You are the apple of His eye, and He has your best interest at heart. Know that your prayers are answered and are conceived in your spirit—just watch for the manifestation. Let's change our countenance and step out in confidence, knowing that our Father loves us and is on our side. As Yolanda Adams sings, 'the battle is not yours, it's the Lord's.' He has already beat the enemy. Victory belongs to you, so own it. The Father loves you. Do you believe it?

Dynamics of Prayer - Part 2

Friday

1 Samuel 2:1-2 (NKJV)

And Hannah prayed and said: "My heart rejoices in the LORD; My horn is exalted in the LORD. I smile at my enemies, because I rejoice in Your salvation. No one is holy like the LORD, For *there is* none besides You, Nor *is there* any rock like our God."

Hannah's prayer for a son was answered. Now, take a look at her prayer of praise. Hannah remembered her distress, just the year before. She was hurt, depressed and felt defeated. But look at her now. The scripture says 'her heart rejoices, her horn is exalted, and she smiles at her enemies. Hannah's confidence rests in her experience of how Jesus fought her battle; Jehovah Jireh answered her call. As you think about Hannah's life, remember two important factors that we can apply to our lives. One, God knows our heart, even better then we know ourselves. Despite her desperation for a son, Hannah endured constant taunting about being barren. Unanswered prayer does not mean God is ignoring us; prayers are answered at God's appointed time. Samuel was not just another male child, but was part of God's plan for the people of Israel.

God has a plan for all of us. When the time is right, our prayers will be answered. The second point of this scripture is how God allowed Hannah to deal with her feelings. Hannah was weary and depressed, and expressed her feelings to the Lord. As believers, we can also cry out to God. There will be times when we don't want to talk to God or anyone else, but we should not stay in that place. After Hannah grieved and did not eat, she finally decided to go to the temple with the belief that her prayer was answered. There comes a time when we have to move from prayer mode to accepting mode, meaning we know that God has our back. He sees the bigger picture, so we need to accept His Word and timing. If you want God's best, wait with expectation and praise. Hannah was not only blessed with Samuel, but was able to have more children. God always does exceedingly and abundantly above all that we can ask or think, and that's a fact. Try Him and see for yourself.

Praying the Scripture

Psalm 119:105 (NKJV)

Your word *is* a lamp to my feet and a light to my path.

When we buy something new, an owner's manual is usually included with the product to ensure we know how it works. The manual lists the features or special functions of the product. Our Creator also provided an owner's manual to help us navigate life via The Bible, or what some have called the 'Basic Instructions Before Leaving Earth.' If we follow the instructions of the Word, we have the ability to make our lives here on Earth purposeful and prosperous. Therefore, it is imperative for us to know the Scriptures and to pray them. The Word of God is a Lamp to our feet and a light to our path. Think about your home when it's dark. A night light gives you just enough light to walk from one room to the other without being completely in the dark. However, there are times when a night light is not sufficient, and a brighter power source is needed. Our lamp, the Word of God, is our guide for daily and everlasting life. We should always pray the scriptures because the Word of God is ALIVE. Take a look:

Hebrews 4:12 (AMP)

For the Word that God speaks is alive and full of power [making it active, operative, energizing, and effective]; it is sharper than any two-edged sword, penetrating to the dividing line of the breath of life (soul) and [the immortal] spirit, and of joints and marrow [of the deepest parts of our nature], exposing *and* sifting *and* analyzing *and* judging the very thoughts and purposes of the heart.

The Amplified Bible translation of this verse is so powerful. The Word of God is so ALIVE and full of POWER that it has the ability to expose our purpose and our deepest thoughts. That is why it's so important to pray 'His will be done' and not our own. Again, God knows us better than we know ourselves. Let's take a look at what Jeremiah says about praying in our own will:

Jeremiah 17:9-10 (NKJV)

"The heart *is* deceitful above all *things,* and desperately wicked; Who can know it?

I, the LORD, search the heart, I test the mind, even to give every man according to his ways, According to the fruit of his doings."

Jeremiah is basically saying that our heart can deceive us. Have you ever seen Christians living in ungodly situations? For example, some living arrangements do not line up with God's Word, but we have convinced ourselves that it is OK. What about people who do not attend church because 'they can do church at home?" The Word makes it very clear that we should regularly assemble ourselves with other believers (Hebrews 10:25). If Jesus went to the synagogue on a daily basis, what example does that set for you and me? The heart can be deceiving. Therefore, we ought to pray, not my will but my Father's will, because no matter how sincere we may think we are, our heart can deceive us. Our Father searches the heart of man and He knows us better than we know ourselves. When we pray for God's will to be done and we obey His will in our lives, we cannot go wrong. In praying the scriptures, we speak life into our situations. Take a look:

Proverbs 18:21 (NKJV)

Death and life *are* in the power of the tongue, and those who love it will eat its fruit.

If life and death is in the power of what we say, then we need to be mindful of how to pray. We should be explicit in prayer, but with the understanding that our prayers may be answered differently than expected.

For example, if you ask God to change a trait about your spouse, perhaps there is something that requires a change in you. Maybe it is God's will for you and your spouse to change—imagine that!

It can be very difficult to pray for individuals as God sees them, rather than our personal feelings about someone. I often hear people say they prayed and prayed for months, even years, for a loved one's salvation. They essentially give up on them when it does not happen within their timeline and chalk it up to, 'they will never accept Christ; they're just lost.' Do you realize that you just tied God's hands with your comment? The Word says in 2 Peter 3:9 that God is patient, not wanting anyone to perish. If we believe what the Word says, we must speak the Word in faith regardless of how long it may take; God's timing is not our timing. What if that person accepts Jesus as their Savior right before they are called to glory? Let's not forget the thief on the cross with Jesus. He accepted Christ right there, and Jesus accepted his repentance and forgave him. We don't know what might happen in a person's life, but God sees and knows every heart. Up to this point, we should remember: the Word of God is ALIVE and full of POWER; the heart is DECEITFUL; DEATH and LIFE is in the power of the tongue.

Take a moment to review the following scriptures, and see how we can incorporate them into our prayer life. When you are afraid, take a look at what Timothy says:

2 Timothy 1:7 (NKJV)

For God has not given us a spirit of fear, but of power and of love and of a sound mind.

Your prayer could go something like this: "Father, I come before you today with fear in my heart, but I know that this is of the enemy. He is trying to deceive me, but you did not give me a spirit of fear; you have given me the power of love and of a sound mind. I thank you that I am more than a conqueror through Christ Jesus." Amen

This is an example of how we conquer fear. The feeling may be present, but feelings are fickle- they come and go-but the Word of God remains the same. If scripture tells us that we weren't given the spirit of fear, then we should stand on His Word.

If you are praying for healing, take a look at this scripture:

Mark 10:27 (NKJV)

But Jesus looked at them and said, "With men *it is* impossible, but not with God; for with God all things are possible."

Your prayer could go something like this:

"Oh Lord, my God, how excellent is your Name. Father, I am praying for healing, because I know that you hold everything in your hand. Your Word says that you can do all things. Nothing is impossible for you, and what doctors cannot do, you can. I'm thankful that by Your stripes, we are healed. Your blood covers every disease; you even conquered death. I thank you Lord in advance for healing my loved one. My trust is in you." Amen.

Do you see why it's so important for us to pray the scriptures? His Word is truth and it cannot lie. We must speak life over our situations. We must remember that regardless of our circumstances, God's Word is our anchor. We stand firm on His Word by walking by faith, and not by sight.

Does this mean that everyone will be healed after prayer? The answer is yes, however the healing may not come in the way you expect. For example, if someone has prayed in faith to walk again, but they remain in a wheelchair, their soul is healed because they received Christ as their Savior. Nothing pleases God more than when we accept Him. When it comes to sickness and disease, sin is the deadliest illness to die in because you are forever doomed. However, dying in Jesus Christ means ultimate healing. So, pray for one's soul to be saved. If we're praying for loved ones that have already accepted Christ, but are still afflicted with physical illnesses, let's review what James says in Chapter 5:14-15:

James 5:14-15 (NKJV)

Is anyone among you sick? Let him call for the elders of the church, and let them pray over him, anointing him with oil in the name of the Lord. And the prayer of faith will save the sick, and the Lord will raise him up. And if he has committed sins, he will be forgiven.

This scripture teaches us that the prayer of faith will heal the sick and raise them up, but it also tells us that sinners who ask for forgiveness will receive it. To be clear, to die in SIN is the deadliest disease. If you are saved, no physical disease can kill your spirit; God can also heal you while on earth, if it is His will. Therefore, when we pray for those who are afflicted with a physical illness, we should believe God will heal them. We are to accept the way He chooses to heal them, whether on earth or in glory, where they are healed forever.

When we pray the Word of God, we can be confident that it will go and perform just what it says it will do, because it cannot return void. When God created this world, He said "let there be," and it was. Again, think of the Word of God as a lamp to our feet and a light to our path. We have the authority, through the power of Jesus Christ, to speak those things that be not as though they were. This does not mean that you can simply 'name it and claim it'. Not so! This speaks to the power of God's promises and how they are fulfilled. For instance, Isaac was born because God made a promise to Abraham. He believed the Word of God, and the promise of a son was fulfilled. He received the son God promised him. Although our faith may waver, like Abraham and Sarah, God's promises never waiver or fail.

God has a plan for your life, and it's a good one. The Word is a roadmap for living. Trust and obey Him, and He will lead you on the path of righteousness. If we commit His Word to our hearts, the Holy Spirit will always guide us when we pray. The more you know the Word, the more the Holy Spirit will speak to you when you pray. As discussed earlier, the Holy Spirit interprets our groaning. Even when we don't know what to say, the Holy Spirit understands our prayer. God operates in truth, while the enemy operates in confusion and chaos. Our Father wants our undivided attention; we should always look to Him.

Praying the scriptures back to God lets us know that our prayers are being heard and answered. Think about this...nothing pleases parents more than hearing their child recall a lesson or guidance provided to them, and then taking it to heart. It is the same with our Heavenly Father. He knows our heart; he knows when we are sincere; He knows when our prayers are self-centered and even dishonest. Hide His Word in your heart, and know that out of your mouth will flow the issues of your heart.

Praying the Scripture

Study Questions & Devotionals

1. Why is it necessary to read the Owner's Manual (Bible)?

   _____

   _____

2. What is the Word of God to our feet?

   _____

   _____

3. What is the light to our path?

   _____

   _____

4. What is the key word in Hebrews 4:12?

   _____

   _____

5. Why should we always pray for God's will rather than our own? (Look at Jeremiah 17:9-10)

   _____

   _____

6. What three things do we learn from Hebrews 4:12, Jeremiah 17:9-10 & Proverbs 18:21?

   _____

   _____

7.   Using 2 Timothy 1:7, write a short prayer in your own words:

_____

_____

8.   In doing this, did God speak to you? Circle one: YES NO

9.   Where does fear stem from?

_____

_____

10. In your own words, what is the difference between what you feel and the Word of God?

_____

_____

11. According to James 5:14-15 what are we to do if there is one among us that is sick?

_____

_____

12. What is the deadliest illness?

_____

_____

13. Did God fulfill His promise to Abraham and Sarah?

_____

_____

14. Did Abraham and Sarah stand on the Word of God?

_____

_____

15. What is the difference of God's timing and our own?

_____

_____

NOTES:

Praying the Scripture

Monday

Psalm 91:9-11 (NKJV)

Because you have made the LORD, *who is* my refuge, *Even* the Most High, your dwelling place. No evil shall befall you, nor shall any plague come near your dwelling; For He shall give His angels charge over you, to keep you in all your ways.

It is through the Word that our Father speaks to us, and we to Him. There are countless promises in His Word for us to pray and to stand on. For every situation, there is a solution. It is imperative to know the Word of God in our heart. Praying His Word is praying His Will. Psalm 91:10-11 is my personal scripture that I pray over my family all the time.

Prayer: "Father thank you for this day you made. I adore you and love you with all my heart. I ask for forgiveness of my sins, those I commit knowingly as well as unknowingly, and I thank you for being a God who is full of grace and mercy. I thank you for protecting my family and loved ones. Father, I thank you that no evil or plague can come near us or our dwelling, because you give the angels charge to keep us in all of our ways. You, oh God, are our provider and protector. Those who dwell in that secret place of the Most High God, and abide under your shadow are covered and protected. I thank you, because you are my King. My family and all connected to me abide in you, therefore they are protected and covered by the blood. Thank you, Father; I love you, and may you perform your will in my life, for your will is perfect." Amen.

Praying the Scripture

Tuesday

Psalm 119:103-105 (NKJV)

How sweet are Your words to my taste, *Sweeter* than honey to my mouth! Through Your precepts I get understanding; Therefore, I hate every false way. Your word *is* a lamp to my feet and a light to my path.

If you're anything like me, I have a sweet tooth, especially for honey—even better if it's locally sourced. Eating a sweet treat is often 'comfort food,' like a slice of apple pie or chocolate cake. Although it's nice to treat ourselves to sweet-tasting goodies every now and then, overindulging in these treats can throw our bodies out of balance. However, there is one sweet indulgence that actually enhances our lives, and that is the Word of God. A serving of the Word provides discernment and understanding of life's situations. Not only are we made aware of God's will through His Word, but the Word illuminates our path—a lamp unto our feet. How can we incorporate this scripture into our prayer life? Start by saying something like this:

Prayer: "Heavenly Father, I'm so grateful to be your child. You chose me way before my parents even thought about me. You are a loving Father, and I love you. Forgive me for any sins I commit against you. Thank you for your wonderful Word; it is sweet to me, and helps me navigate through life's situations. It soothes my heart when I'm in trouble and guides my feet so that I will not stumble. Not only does your Word provide clarity about what is happening now, but you help me to make decisions that affect my future. You are God Almighty, who sees and knows all. May your will be done. Thank you for this day, and allowing me to take part in it." Amen.

Praying the Scripture Devotional

Wednesday

Proverbs 18:20-21 (NKJV)

A man's stomach shall be satisfied from the fruit of his mouth; From the produce of his lips he shall be filled. Death and life *are* in the power of the tongue, and those who love it will eat its fruit.

It's the middle of the week. Are you feeling more comfortable about praying the scriptures? We must remember that God's Word is alive. Let me explain what I mean by this. I'm sure you have read the 23rd Psalm over and over again. But, perhaps you're having a day when you truly feel like you're in the valley—life has thrown you a curve ball, and you are feeling down and out. In that moment, reading Psalm 23 feels different because it personally speaks to you. You may identify with David's account of God's comfort and protection. You are not afraid; you realize that this valley is just a shadow, and that the Father has been leading you the entire time. Take another look at our scripture for today: A man's stomach is satisfied from the fruit of his mouth, meaning the words we utter from our lips are very important. We have authority through our tongue. So when we say, "I'm not going to have a good day today," we've basically sealed the deal. Guess what? We will probably have the day we declared through this dead statement. Instead swap out the former statement with this one: "This is the day that the Lord has made; I am glad and I choose to rejoice today. This will be a productive day." Do you see the difference? Friends, we can look at the glass as half empty or half full. Personally, I like my glass half full.

Prayer: "Father, I know that there is power in your Word. Help me to speak life not death. May the fruit of my mouth always satisfy my stomach. Help me to speak wholesome, healthy words to all I come in contact with. In the Name of Jesus, my wonderful Savior, I pray." Amen.

Praying the Scripture

Thursday

James 5:14-15 (NKJV)

Is anyone among you sick? Let him call for the elders of the church, and let them pray over him, anointing him with oil in the name of the Lord. And the prayer of faith will save the sick, and the Lord will raise him up. And if he has committed sins, he will be forgiven.

There is nothing God cannot heal, no sickness or disease that He can't cure. Will God heal everyone we pray for? Yes, but not in the way we may expect Him to. First and foremost, we must understand that God's will is perfect. Second, we need to understand that there is no greater illness than SIN. If one is not saved and die, you are forever lost. There is no physical illness worst then being lost in sin. Hell is a real place for those who refuse to accept Jesus. Physical illness is a part of life, and The Bible tells us that the body will decay. Some will be healed on earth, and others be healed when joined with the Father. As believers, our job is to pray for the sick- whether we call the elders or deacons of the church- or if we pray individually. The prayer of faith will save the sick and it is the Lord that will raise the sick from their sick bed. Anointing someone with oil is a representation of the Holy Spirit.

Our prayers should always be Spirit-led and Spirit-filled. We often question individuals who have suffered from physical illnesses all of their lives, and we wonder why. Although we don't always understand the 'why,' I know God uses them in mighty ways. Other individuals have experienced miraculous healings and again, God uses them. Moral of the story… be encouraged in knowing that our Father makes no mistakes, and pray for those that are sick among us. Believe that God's will is perfect. Every day is a miracle, and every form of healing is perfect, whether on earth or in heaven. Glory to the matchless name of God-Jehovah Rapha, our Healer.

Praying the Scripture Devotional

Friday

Mark 10:27 (NKJV)

But Jesus looked at them and said, "With men *it is* impossible, but not with God; for with God all things are possible."

What a wonderful week this has been! I began this week by sharing one of my favorite scriptures, Psalm 91. I pray this over my family and friends all the time. I know without a doubt that God's Word is alive, because He has proven it to me time and time again. Let His Word be a lamp to your feet that guides you through life's circumstances, so you will not stumble or fall. Speak life over dead situations. We have been given authority through the power of Jesus Christ, but we must pray believing that with God, all things are possible. Nothing is too hard for our Father; He is omniscient, omnipresent and omnipotent. 'All things work together for the good of those who love Him, who have been called according to His purpose" (Romans 8:28 NIV). My dear friends, let the Word saturate your hearts, and watch the Father reveal Himself to you in ways you've never imagined.

Prayer: "Father, I thank you for this week. Thank you for teaching and leading me. Your Word is sweeter than honey from a honeycomb. Thank you for lighting my path so that I will not stumble or fall. Thank you for reassuring me that we are never alone, and that all things are possible with you. Help me to always keep my eyes on you. Thank you for Jesus, and the Holy Spirit within me, who leads me to all truth. How excellent is Your Holy Name, which is above all names. One day, every knee will bow, and every tongue will confess, that Jesus is Lord. I love you, Father." Amen.

Meditating the Scripture

Joshua 1:8 (NKJV)

This Book of the Law shall not depart from your mouth, but you shall meditate in it day and night that you may observe to do according to all that is written in it. For then you will make your way prosperous, and then you will have good success.

Do you ever feel like your prayer life is monotonous? I'm sure we all have at some point in time. We often ask, "God, are you listening? Do you hear me? Why haven't you answered my prayers?" I'm sure the prophets from the Bible felt the same way, given God's 400-year silence between the books of Malachi and Matthew. However, God still spoke to individuals during this time, just not in the way you might expect. For example, in Numbers 22, God used a donkey to speak to Balaam. The donkey attempted to get Balaam's attention on three occasions. Balaam kept striking the donkey for not moving, until it was revealed that the donkey finally said (paraphrased): "why are you beating me, when all I'm doing is keeping you from getting killed?" You see, the donkey saw the angel and tried to warn him. God often speaks, but it's us who fail to listen because He might not speak the way we expect Him to.

This is why prayer is the foundation of our daily walk. It's essential that we communicate with our Maker. Meditating through scripture is one sure way to hear God speak. Meditation can be defined as "written or spoken discourse expressing considerate thought on a subject." Let's look at how meditation is referenced in the Hebrew and Greek languages. In Hebrew, the word *hagah* means to "muse", "growl", "moan", and "utter". We can see through the following scriptures how meditation is manifested in several ways. For example, in Joshua 1:8, believers are instructed to meditate on

God's word as a source of inspiration and creativity. Job 27:4 says "…my tongue will utter no deceit." Jeremiah 48:31 says, "Therefore I wail over Moab, for all Moab I cry out…" (NIV). The Hebrew word for muse or *suach* is defined as being "bowed down" or "downcast" or "full of despair." In Genesis 24, Isaac was promised by God- through his father, Abraham- the promise of a wife. This chapter details how Abraham's servant was to identify a worthy wife for Isaac. Verses 63 and 64 shows how Isaac put his faith into action: "He went out to the field one evening to meditate, and as he looked up, he saw camels approaching. Rebekah also looked up and saw Isaac." The remainder of the chapter shows the servant explaining to Isaac how Rebekah had fulfilled God's prophesy via Abraham.

The Greek word for mediation is *meletao*, "to care for, "attend to carefully" or to "practice." In Timothy 4:13-15, meditation is described as immersing ourselves into the Word of God: "Until I come, devote yourself to the public reading of Scripture, to preaching and to teaching." It is very important to not only pray the scriptures, but to meditate in the scriptures as well. Here are a few more reasons why we should meditate on the Word of God, as shown in Psalms 119: 9-11:

Psalm 119:9-11ESV: How can a young man keep his way pure? By guarding it according to your word. With my whole heart I seek you; let me not wander from your commandments! I have stored up your word in my heart that I might not sin against you.

We must guard our hearts based on God's Word. When we wholeheartedly seek God, we should always compare our situations to the Word. How do we know if something is right or wrong? By comparing it to the Word. If you are not sure about something, seek God and you will find Him. Meditate on the scriptures He lays on your heart, and wait until you have peace in your spirit. God is not the author of confusion. Remember the world has its version of what is true, but God is the truth.

Romans 12:2ESV: Do not be conformed to this world, but be transformed by the renewal of your mind, that by testing you may discern what is the will of God, what is good and acceptable and perfect.

Our minds can only be renewed if we meditate on the Word of God, and allow it to sink deep into our spirit. Remember this, whatever we allow in will eventually come out! I have a saying: "Trash in, trash will certainly come out; Word of God in, and Word of God will come out." So, brothers and sisters, what are you meditating (thinking) about as you go about your day? Here's what God says:

Philippians 4:8ESV: Finally, brothers, whatever is true, whatever is honorable, whatever is just, whatever is pure, whatever is lovely, whatever is commendable, if there is any excellence, if there is anything worthy of praise, think about these things.

In other words, instead of cluttering our minds with garbage, think on the Word of God. It renews our minds, and remains a lamp unto our feet. Don't allow worry, jealousy, or envy to fill up your thoughts. The Word of God should consume us to the point that we'll be amazed about how much better our lives will become; it is because we are submitting ourselves to The One who gave us life. He knows us better than we know ourselves. Our Father has a plan for us, and it is not to harm us, but to help us grow in Him. Therefore, we should be mindful about what we're thinking about. What is consuming our thoughts? If our thoughts don't line up with Philippians 4:8, we might need to throw out some stuff. When our thinking is cluttered, we can't find God. Take time to de-clutter your mind, meditate on the Word of God, and watch what happens in your Spirit man.

MEDITATING THE SCRIPTURES

Study Questions & Devotionals

1. What book of the Law is Joshua making reference to?

   _____

   _____

2. Do you ever feel like your prayers are monotonous? Explain.

   _____

   _____

3. How many years passed before God spoke between the OT book of Malachi and the NT book of Matthew?

   _____

   _____

4. What animal did God use in Numbers 22 to speak to Balaam?

   _____

   _____

Look up the following scriptures and describe which form of meditation is used in each of them: Job 27:4; Jeremiah 48:31; Genesis 24:63; 1 Timothy 4:13-15

Hagah – muse, growl, moan and utter

Suach – muse

Meletao – to care for, practice study

Job 27:4

_____

Jeremiah 48:31

_____

Genesis 24:63

_____

1 Timothy 4:13-15

_____

5. How can we keep our way pure?

_____

_____

6. How can we renew our mind, by being conformed or transformed?

_____

_____

7. According to Philippians 4:8, what are some things we should think about?

_____

_____

8. Why is it important to think about what we are thinking about?

_____

_____

9. What is the best way to replace worldly thoughts?

    _____

    _____

10. What do we find in God's Word?

    _____

    _____

NOTES:

Meditating the Scripture Devotional

Monday

My dear friends of God: In studying this week's lesson, we learned the importance of meditating the Scriptures, and now is your opportunity to practice what you've learned. Think about a scripture, write it down on a sticky note, and place it around you. Whenever you need a reminder of His promises, just lean on the scripture(s) throughout the day. Listen to the Holy Spirit, keep a journal of your thoughts, and watch over time what the Holy Spirit speaks into your spirit. Your journal will help you share your testimony with others. Enjoy your time with the Father. Let us begin with our opening scripture:

Joshua 1:8 (NKJV)

This Book of the Law shall not depart from your mouth, but you shall meditate in it day and night that you may observe to do according to all that is written in it. For then you will make your way prosperous, and then you will have good success.

As you meditate, jot down what the Holy Spirit is saying to you. This scripture says to me, the more I meditate, the more God will write them on my heart. Therefore, in my time of need, I don't have to have a Bible in hand for God's Word to burst out of me. I also hear the Holy Spirit saying that just in knowing the Word will lead me to prosper in all I do; it will cause me to have success in life. God has a plan and His plan is for our good. I will meditate in His marvelous word day and night. Joshua 1:8 reminds me of Isaiah 43:2:

Isaiah 43:2NKJV: When you pass through the waters, I will be with you; and through the rivers, they shall not overflow you. When you walk through the fire, you shall not be burned, nor shall the flame scorch you.

When we mediate in God's Word, it leads us to acknowledge and worship what a mighty God we serve! He is our Majesty. How excellent is His Name; Hallelujah to the precious Lamb of God.

Meditating the Scripture Devotional

Tuesday

Psalm 119:9-11ESV: How can a young man keep his way pure? By guarding it according to your word. With my whole heart I seek you; let me not wander from your commandments! I have stored up your word in my heart that I might not sin against you.

As we meditate on Psalm 119:9-11, let us think about how we can keep our heart pure. There is but one way… we must guard our heart according to the Word. How can we do this? With our whole hearts, we must seek Him and constantly do an internal gut check. Personally, there are times when I'm seeking God with everything I have, and other times when I have not. When I am half-heartedly seeking God, I allow other things to creep in and get in the way. The writer goes on to say, "Let me not wander away from your commandments." Sometimes the cares of the world make it so easy to wander away. However, we should be reminded of Psalm 23:4KJV: "Yea, though I walk through the valley of the shadow of death I will fear no evil." Why? Because the Lord is my Shepherd and He is with me; His rod and staff, they comfort me. At times, we're all like lost sheep. We wander off, but the gentle rod of the Shepherd leads us safely back to the flock. As the Word says, when ninety-nine sheep are accounted for and one is missing, the Shepherd will not stop until He brings the lost sheep back in. Just remember when we're lost, our Shepherd loves us too much to allow us to continue wandering around for long. The more we're in the Word, the less we wander off. With our whole heart, let us seek you, Lord. I love you, Father.

Meditating the Scripture Devotional

Wednesday

Romans 12:2ESV: Do not be conformed to this world, but be transformed by the renewal of your mind, that by testing you may discern what is the will of God, what is good and acceptable and perfect.

This is one of my many favorite scriptures to meditate on. Think about it, we are in the world every day, so it's easy to get entangled in worldly things. This scripture reminds me that though I am *in* the world, I'm not *of* the world. As you go through your day, ask yourself, "am I conforming or transforming? Maybe you are at work, and some of your co-workers are talking about another co-worker, or even the boss. What do *you* do? Do you join the conversation? Do you just stand by and listen? Do you speak up, letting your co-workers know that it's wrong to talk about someone in a negative way? Or do you remove yourself from the conversation by walking away? What is the will of God in that situation? What do you discern? I must confess, there have been times in my life when I would join right in and gossip along with the best of them. As I learned more about God's Word, I began to be quiet and just listen, telling myself that as long as I don't participate in the conversation, I'm not doing anything wrong. Eventually, I got to the point where I would remove myself from conversations, but then the Holy Spirit would convict me that I should have spoken up, which made me uncomfortable. I did not want to do it; I was worried about what people would think of me. The more I meditated on the Word, the more the Father transformed my mind. I'm still a work in progress, but I thank my Father for always teaching me.

As I stay in the Word, my mind is constantly being renewed. When I feel led to speak up, I no longer worry about what one might think. With a loving spirit, I let people in my sphere know when conversations are going in the wrong direction. I strive to discern what the will of God is, and what is good, acceptable and perfect in His sight. It is my heart's desire to be in His perfect will. How about you? Let the Word transform and renew your mind.

Meditating the Scripture Devotional

Thursday

Philippians 4:8ESV: Finally, brothers, whatever is true, whatever is honorable, whatever is just, whatever is pure, whatever is lovely, whatever is commendable, if there is any excellence, if there is anything worthy of praise, think about these things.

Do you ever think about your thoughts? I often ask this question because very seldom do we think about the thoughts that run through our mind on any given day. However, when we take time to meditate, we're engaging in focused thinking. Meditation teaches us to think about *what* we are thinking about. In today's devotional, Paul's letter to the Philippians encourages us to stay united, joyful, and in prayer. In verse 8, Paul is basically saying, "Sisters and Brothers, think about what you are thinking about. Set your mind on things that are sincere, ethical, fair and impartial. Whatever is uncontaminated, whatever is lovely, whatever is praiseworthy, admirable-if there is any greatness, if there is anything worthy of praise-these are the things that should occupy our minds."

As I meditated on today's scripture, I simply swapped out Paul's words with a couple of synonyms to truly understand his words. I encourage you to do the same with all passages of scripture, so you can better apply the teachings to your life. *Think* about what you are thinking about. Constantly ask yourself, "are my thoughts pure, true, honorable, and commendable, etc.?" If your answer is no, make purposefully changes to correct your thoughts. The Bible tells us to "cast down imaginations, and every high thing that exalts itself against the knowledge of God, and bringing into captivity every thought to the obedience of Christ." (2 Corinthians 10:5 KJV) My dear friends, we have the power to control our thinking by purposefully meditating on the Word of God.

Meditating the Scripture Devotional

Friday

We have arrived at the end of the week. Take a moment to reflect on the devotionals from the beginning of the week. Did you take some time to write out your thoughts? Have you allowed the Holy Spirit to speak to you? Are you now more comfortable with meditation? Friends, it's not rocket science to meditate; it simply takes focused thinking. When there is something important to remember, begin with that thought on your mind. You may write the task down, or set a reminder on your smartphone. Whether it is picking up a prescription, or going to the grocery store for an ingredient for tonight's dinner, focusing on important tasks remains at the forefront of your mind throughout the day. We must approach the same tactics when meditating on God's Word. Here is the final scripture that you should meditate on until you know it by heart:

1 Thessalonians 5:16-19 (NKJV)

Rejoice always, pray without ceasing, in everything give thanks; for this is the will of God in Christ Jesus for you. Do not quench the Spirit.

Friends, when you write the Word on your heart, no one is able to take that away from you. When you wake up in the morning, we should rejoice for having breath in our bodies. Pray without ceasing, by talking with the Father throughout your day. Regardless of the situation, thank God for keeping you in His perfect will. Please note, it does not say "*for* everything, give thanks," but "*in* everything, give thanks." As slight as it sounds, there is a difference. Many have misinterpreted this by thinking God wants us to be thankful for bad things—quite the contrary! God is saying we always have something to be thankful for by listening to the Holy Spirit. He is here to guide us in truth. Write the scriptures on your heart by meditating on them. Whoever believes in Jesus, according to the scriptures, will have rivers of living water flowing from within. Remember, what you put in will come out. If you feed yourself with the Word, then the Word will come out. What are you chewing on today?

Monologue vs. Dialogue

This teaching focuses on talking and listening to God. As I was preparing for this section, I noticed that *monologue* is defined as "a long speech by one person during a conversation," while a *dialogue* is a "conversation between two or more people." The common denominator in both terms involves listening, which reminds me of James 1:19, where we are directed to be quick to listen and slow to speak. God gave us two ears and one mouth, yet most of us speak more than we listen. I love to talk! However, over the years I've also learned to listen. As a licensed cosmetologist, I often feel like a psychologist, counselor, or therapist. My clients, who have become more like friends and family, seem very comfortable discussing their personal issues with me. I'm thankful to the Father because my profession is also ministry, in that I'm afforded the opportunity to minister to my clients just by listening to them, or praying for and with them. More importantly, my clients know when they talk to me, everything stays with me, only traveling to the Father's ear.

It is also important for us to listen to God through the Holy Spirit, which means drawing from within. Don't get me wrong, God can speak to us by any method, even an audible voice. He spoke to Moses through a burning bush; He spoke to Joseph through dreams and visions; Jesus spoke through various prophets. If God can use a donkey to get one's attention, we know that He can speak in all kinds of ways. However, God most often speaks to us through the Holy Spirit, which is why it is so important to be still, as Psalms 46:10 says. In being still, we can hear from God. If we are constantly surrounded by noise and chatter, it's hard to hear anything, much less God.

In previous lessons, we discussed meditating on the Word of God and praying the scriptures, which are all important aspects in our walk. However, as we read the Word, are we truly feeding our soul? Take a look at Jeremiah 15:16:

Jeremiah 15:16 (NKJV)

Your words were found, and I ate them, And Your word was to me the joy and rejoicing of my heart; For I am called by Your name, O LORD God of hosts.

There are times when we become so intent on mastering theories and theologies of the Word of God, so that we appear more holy or intelligent to others. The purpose of reading the Bible is about developing a closer relationship with God. Studying the Word of God does not automatically grant us eternal life; we must repent and accept Jesus Christ as our Savior. Therefore, we must move beyond just reading the Word of God for information, but to meditate in the Word for our daily living. Again, it is in the quietness of meditation that the Holy Spirit often speaks to us. The problem is our prayers are often monologuing rather than dialogues with God. Have your prayers been similar to this?

"Father in heaven, thank you for all you've done for me. Today, I come asking for healing, and I pray that you help me out of this situation I got myself into. Please watch over my kids as they go to school. I pray that you will also go by the nursing home and check on my mother, since I won't have time to go there today. Please feed the hungry and cloth the homeless. Thank you, God, for all you do." Amen.

Can you identify with this way of praying? The above prayer is an example of a monologue. Too often, our prayers are more like a "to-do" list or wish list of wants to God. We're sending God our list of errands, instead of leaving room for God to speak to us. The above example is not to make fun of or belittle anyone about how you may pray. It is about acknowledging that while we make our petition before God, we should also wait and anticipate a response from Him as well. In the early days of the weekly prayer group, our prayers were just like this. When I listen to our prayers now, I can clearly see how much our prayers have changed. We still make our requests known to the Father, but believe me, we now listen for direction from the Holy Spirit, which then leads us into adoration and worship. God wants our attention by staying in His presence.

In John 10, Jesus is described as a Shepherd, and His followers as sheep. Sheep have a tendency to wander, but the Shepherd knows how to get our attention when we stray away from the flock. Friends, let us practice listening for the voice of the Shepherd. We should begin prayer by asking God to speak to us, then let Him know our concerns. After we are finished praying, don't walk away immediately; wait on God to speak.

To be clear, we will not all hear the Father speak in the same way. Let me share a few ways you may experience God's voice, as you learn to tarry in His presence. Depending on what you are praying for determines how you will hear His voice. Perhaps hearing from God takes the form of having a feeling of peace after praying; you have a peace in knowing God is there and heard you speak. Have you ever been led by the Holy Spirit to read a particular scripture, and the answer to your prayer is right there? Or maybe you believed God to be leading you in one direction, only to be prompted by the Holy Spirit to go in a completely different direction? Another way God may speak to you is through revelation, which may come via a dream or prophesy.

God can also speak to us in an audible voice, whether He speaks directly to us or communicates through a surrogate. The surrogate may be a person or an object. In Genesis, God spoke directly to Adam and Eve; in Exodus, God spoke to Moses from a burning bush; God spoke to Israel from Mount Sinai; God used a blinding light to get Saul's attention; John, the revelator, heard a loud voice that sounded like a trumpet, only to realize it was Jesus. Peter saw Jesus in a vision. When Jesus was baptized, God directly said, "this is my beloved Son, in whom I am well pleased." Throughout the Word, we see God using various means to reach His people. Regardless of the method, God has a way of speaking to us so we can recognize His voice. God is the same yesterday, today and forevermore. He does not change. When He needs to get in touch with you, trust me, He knows how to find you-- no social media, phone, or email required. Wait on the Father, and He will give you direction.

MONOLOGUE VERSES DIALOGUE

Study Questions

1. What is the difference between monologue and dialogue?

_____

_____

_____

_____

2. What is the common denominator between monologue and dialogue?

_____

_____

3. James 1:19 tells us to be quick to listen, slow to speak, and slow to do what?

_____

_____

4. In Jeremiah 15:16, the writer says that he ate the Word. What does that mean to you?

_____

_____

_____

_____

5. How does God speak to you?

_____

_____

_____

_____

6. Describe your prayers from when you first were saved to now. Do you see a change?

_____

_____

_____

_____

7. How do the sheep know the Shepherd?

_____

_____

8. Does God speak to all of us the same way?

_____

_____

9. What are some ways God may use to speak to us?

_____

_____

_____

_____

10. What is the key to hearing God speak?

_____

_____

11. Take a moment to pray, listen to what God has said to you, and then write down it down.

_____

_____

_____

_____

Notes:

Monologue Verses Dialogue Devotional

Monday

This week, I will share prayers from the Word of God. I charge you to read them, and relate them to your personal situations. Listen to the Holy Spirit and jot down what you hear; in other words, wait for a response or dialogue. Let's begin with David's prayer, after realizing he sinned against God with Bathsheba. David humbled himself before God, which is something we all should do before going before the throne of grace.

Psalm 51:2-4, 7, 10-12 (NKJV)

"Wash me thoroughly from my iniquity, and cleanse me from my sin. For I acknowledge my transgressions, and my sin *is* always before me. Against You, you only, have I sinned, and done *this* evil in Your sight-- That You may be found just when You speak, *and* blameless when You judge. Purge me with hyssop, and I shall be clean; wash me, and I shall be whiter than snow. Create in me a clean heart, O God, and renew a steadfast spirit within me. Do not cast me away from Your presence, and do not take Your Holy Spirit from me. Restore to me the joy of Your salvation, and uphold me by Your generous Spirit."

What do you hear God saying to you?

_____

_____

_____

_____

Monologue Verses Dialogue Devotional

Tuesday

Yesterday, we learned about praying humbly for forgiveness of our sins, which is an essential part of prayer. Today, we'll look at how prayer is focused on receiving guidance. David was a king. Despite his authority, David knew the importance of seeking counsel from God. You and I need to be led by our Heavenly Father every day. Let's see what David asked for:

Psalm 25:1-2, 4-6 (HCSB)

LORD, I turn to You. My God, I trust in You. Do not let me be disgraced; do not let my enemies gloat over me. Make Your ways known to me, LORD; teach me Your paths. Guide me in Your truth and teach me, for You are the God of my salvation; I wait for You all day long. Remember, LORD, Your compassion and Your faithful love, for they [have existed] from antiquity.

God has a plan for you and me; it is not to harm us but to do us good. What is the Holy Spirit saying to you as you pray this prayer?

_____

_____

_____

_____

_____

_____

_____

_____

_____

_____

Monologue Verses Dialogue Devotional

Wednesday

By far, The Lord's prayer is the most popular prayer on earth. Most believers were taught to memorize it as a child, or upon accepting Christ as your Savior. This is a powerful prayer that provides instructions on how to approach our Father. It teaches us to forgive in order to be forgiven. It also provides security about who can deliver us from evil. If you don't know what to pray, this is the perfect prayer for you; it covers everything!

Matthew 6:9-13 (ESV)

Pray then like this: "Our Father in heaven, hallowed be your name. Your kingdom come, your will be done, on earth as it is in heaven. Give us this day our daily bread, and forgive us our debts, as we also have forgiven our debtors. And lead us not into temptation, but deliver us from evil.

What does the Lord's Prayer mean to you?

_____

_____

_____

_____

_____

_____

_____

_____

_____

Monologue Verses Dialogue Devotional

Thursday

In Colossians 1:9-14, Paul prayed for the church as a whole. Although he never met the Colossians' personally, Paul was still compelled to pray for them. Like Paul, we are called to pray for one another.

Colossians 1:9-14 (ESV)

And so, from the day we heard, we have not ceased to pray for you, asking that you may be filled with the knowledge of his will in all spiritual wisdom and understanding, so as to walk in a manner worthy of the Lord, fully pleasing to him, bearing fruit in every good work and increasing in the knowledge of God. May you be strengthened with all power, according to his glorious might, for all endurance and patience with joy, giving thanks to the Father, who has qualified you to share in the inheritance of the saints in light. He has delivered us from the domain of darkness and transferred us to the kingdom of his beloved Son, in whom we have redemption, the forgiveness of sins.

What is the Holy Spirit saying to you in this passage?

_____

_____

_____

_____

_____

_____

_____

_____

_____

Monologue Verses Dialogue Devotional

Friday

How are you coming along with your prayer time? Are your prayers more of a dialogue or a monologue? Are you writing down what the Holy Spirit says to you after you pray? Today, create your own prayer, using what you have learned so far. Don't forget to pray and meditate on the scriptures, then apply it here.

_____

_____

_____

_____

_____

_____

_____

Now listen to what the Holy Spirit is saying to you.

_____

_____

_____

_____

_____

_____

_____

Amen, Amen, and Amen.

Pray, Watch & Wait

How do we attempt to combat Satan and his demons? There is but one way, and that is through prayer. There is a saying, "no prayer, no power; little prayer, little power; much prayer, ALL power." In other words, the more we pray, the more we know what to do. There is a verse of a children's song that says: "Your heart is like a garden, where Jesus plants His seeds. Watch out, so Satan doesn't come and plant some ugly weeds."

How befitting this little verse is to our lives. We are created to worship and adore our Father, but Satan's goal is to destroy this connection. He wants us to bow down to him, so he plants ugly weeds (thoughts) in our gardens to try and kill our communication with God. Our hearts are like the garden; what our hearts produce depends on the amount of time we spend with the Gardener. When we pray, watch and wait, we can prevent weeds from growing. Think about this…a person who consistently maintains their flower beds will see a weed as soon as it sprouts up. On the other hand, if you tend to your flower beds every now and then, it takes significantly more time to pull the weeds out. The longer the weeds are left to grow, the deeper the roots. Eventually, the weeds crowd out the flowers, and infiltrate the entire flower bed.

It is the same way with our prayer life, if you spend time with the Father on a daily basis, you will be less likely to enter into temptation. Take a look at what Jesus said to some of His disciples:

Matthew 26:41 (ESV)

Watch and pray that you may not enter into temptation. The spirit indeed is willing, but the flesh is weak."

Jesus was asking His disciples to watch and pray, not for His sake, but for themselves. Notice He says, "so that you may not enter into temptation." The Greek word for *watch* is *gregopeo* meaning to "be vigilant, be alert, and to keep your eyes open." With temptation lurking on every side, Jesus commands us to be alert, and to remain spiritually awake. We often have good intentions to do what is right, but even our best intentions can be overpowered if we become lax in our walk with God. Perhaps you heard the saying, "starve the flesh and feed the spirit?" Whatever you give the most attention to will grow. If we are constantly tending to the flesh, our spirit will suffer. We need to be on the lookout for anything distracting our relationship with God. Jesus told the disciples to simply watch and pray with Him; this was the night before His crucifixion in the garden of Gethsemane.

This reminds me of a time when Perky, one of my prayer partners and dear friend, decided to reserve a hotel room to devote some time for serious prayer. We wanted to hear from the Lord, with no phones, children or spouses to distract us. The plan was to pray all night and to wait to hear from the Holy Spirit. We decided to get something to eat, so we would not have to leave the room once we checked in. If you know Perky and I, we love to eat! At the restaurant, we began ordering all kinds of food, and everything was delicious. Needless to say, when we were done, we were good and full. We arrived at the hotel, checked in, and proceeded to get comfortable, because we wanted nothing to disturb us during our prayer time. Little did we know, our spirits were willing, but our flesh were weak. After freshening up, I found Perky sound asleep on her bed. I tried waking her up, with no luck. I attempted to carry on with prayer, and even said to myself, "the enemy is not going to defeat our purpose for coming here." Well, that lasted a whopping 15-30 minutes! The next thing I know, I was waking up to daylight.

Friends, in our walk with Christ, we must always be alert and aware of the snares of the world. We must stay on the lookout for anything on this earth that takes us away from our relationship with God. Why? Take a look at 1 Peter:

1 Peter 5:8 (NKJV)

Be sober, be vigilant, because your adversary, the devil, walks about like a roaring lion, seeking whom he may devour.

In this passage, Peter tells the crowd to avoid being drunk, not with alcohol, but through the dulling of our soul. Although alcohol dulls our senses, allowing the concerns of the world to overtake our souls can have the same effect. In other words, never let your guard down. Peter then says Satan "walks about like a roaring lion, seeking whom he may devour." An adversary is an opponent in a conflict or dispute. Think about this, the enemy is always making noise, attempting to destroy us. The text says Satan is like a lion, meaning his role is to scare and distract us. His roar is not real; it may be loud, but that's about it—a bunch of noise. However, do not underestimate his effectiveness in tempting us. The adversary comes to oppose everything Godly we stand for. He comes to persecute us to death, especially if he can persuade us to go his way.

Satan is also cunning. He presents himself as a serpent to attract our senses, to pervert our judgement, and to captivate our imagination. He also portrays himself as an angel of light, attempting to deceive us with false religion. He takes what is spiritual and twists it; he'll take what is pure and defiles it. He also wants us to think it's ok to kill or hurt others. If Satan can take ungodly things to make them appear righteous, then he has you. Satan constantly looks for prey; if you get caught with your guard down, he has no mercy. He also weaves himself into issues to divide us, by keeping disagreements and contention in the forefront, instead of being united through Jesus Christ. In Christ, we are one; there are no big I's and little U's.

This is why praying, watching and waiting enables us to recognize the various disguises the enemy uses. Hopefully, we'll be able to distinguish between infused light vs. real light. Let's pray we are able to recognize the difference between true religion and fake religion, and err on the side of Jesus Christ. I'm so glad that I know the real Lion, the Lion of the tribe of Judah; the Root of David; the conqueror of the last enemy called death, for only the Father knows the day or hour when we shall behold His return. Every knee will bow, for He is the Alpha and the Omega, the beginning and the end. There will be no more pain and anguish, no more depression and certainly no more of the enemy's schemes. Satan will be destroyed once and for all. All the Saints will gather around the throne of God worshiping Him, because He is worthy of all the praise and glory.

PRAY WATCH & WAIT

Study Questions & Devotionals

1. What does it mean to watch and pray?

    _____

    _____

2. What can we do to keep our flesh from getting weak?

    _____

    _____

3. What does it mean to be sober and vigilant?

    _____

    _____

4. Define the word adversary.

    _____

    _____

5. What three disguises does the enemy use?

    _____

    _____

    _____

    _____

6. As a roaring lion, he comes to do what?

   _____

   _____

7. As an angel of light, he comes to do what?

   _____

   _____

8. As the serpent, he comes to do what?

   _____

   _____

9. In your own words, why should you pray, watch, and wait?

   _____

   _____

10. What does praying, watching and waiting help you recognize?

    _____

    _____

11. Recall a time when your spirit was willing, but the flesh was weak.

    _____

    _____

    _____

    _____

Notes:

Pray, Watch, & Wait Devotional

Monday

This week's devotionals are based on the principles we learned about praying, watching and waiting to hear from God. Let's take a look at Mark 13.

Mark 13:33-37 (NKJV) Take heed, watch and pray; for you do not know when the time is. *It is* like a man going to a far country, who left his house and gave authority to his servants, and to each his work, and commanded the doorkeeper to watch. Watch therefore, for you do not know when the master of the house is coming--in the evening, at midnight, at the crowing of the rooster, or in the morning-- lest, coming suddenly, he finds you sleeping. And what I say to you, I say to all: Watch!

What if you were one of the servants in the above scripture? The owner of the house has placed a lot of responsibility upon his servants. The doorkeeper has a very important role, serving as the first line of defense in guarding the home while the master is out. The text says the doorkeeper must stay on guard because the master can return at any time. Have you heard the saying, "when the boss is away, the mice play?" The question is, what are you doing when no one is looking? More importantly, what will you be doing when Jesus returns? No man knows the time or day, but we do know that Jesus will return.

As doorkeepers, are we watching and praying? Every day should be a dress rehearsal for His return. Think about this...what would you be doing if you knew the Lord was coming today? I'm sure we would begin preparing for Jesus's arrival months in advance; we would make sure everything was in place. Since we don't know when Jesus will return, we must *stay* ready, so we don't have to *get* ready. We can stand guard by reading and studying His Word, discerning good from evil, and remaining faithful to His will. Watch and pray, so when the Master returns, we are prepared to go with Him to paradise.

Pray, Watch, & Wait Devotional

Tuesday

Luke 21:34-36 (NKJV): But take heed to yourselves, lest your hearts be weighed down with carousing, drunkenness, and cares of this life, and that Day come on you unexpectedly. For it will come as a snare on all those who dwell on the face of the whole earth. Watch therefore, and pray always that you may be counted worthy to escape all these things that will come to pass, and to stand before the Son of Man.

In this passage, Jesus warns the disciples about focusing on the cares of the world, which diverts our attention away from Him. We are currently in the midst of a global pandemic, COVID-19. This virus came upon us out of nowhere, and has impacted the entire world. Were we prepared for this? Absolutely not! Nevertheless, we can prepare for the Lord's return. We have an advantage, in that the life instructions are right before us via the Word of God (Bible). Though we don't know when Jesus will return, we know for a fact that He will. Jesus wanted the disciples to avoid the trappings of the world so they could stand before the Son of Man. So, what are we watching out for? SIN. If we let our guard down, we can so easily enter into sin. If we keep our eyes on God, we will remain rooted and grounded.

We should not only watch out for sin, but we can seek out opportunities to do the Father's work by spreading the Word of God to those in darkness. The Father does not want anyone to perish, so while we are here, it is our duty as Christian brothers and sisters to pray for the salvation of the lost. We must share the story about Jesus Christ to others, so they may see Jesus in us. We must strive to love one another regardless of where we are from, what we look like, what color we are, or what race we are. God loves all of His children and we should too. We must realize in not liking someone because they look different, is not only racism, but sin. Pray, Watch and Wait on the Lord, for He is coming back with a shout, and every eye will behold Him. Are you ready?

Pray, Watch, & Wait Devotional

Wednesday

1 Peter 5:8 (NKJV): Be sober, be vigilant; because your adversary the devil walks about like a roaring lion, seeking whom he may devour.

This is a short, but powerful verse. Let's break down some of the words in this passage. *Sober* means "clearheaded;" *vigilant* means "watchful;" *adversary* is another word for "enemy;" *devour* means to "destroy." Peter is telling us to be clear headed, because the enemy's desire is to destroy us, by any means necessary. The enemy sets traps so we may fall. 2 Timothy also says to be sober-minded and to endure suffering. This means that although we will have trials and tribulations here on earth, our Father promised never to leave or forsake us. He is always by our side. We must be careful to not conform to the world, but to test all things so we can discern the will of God for our lives. Sin lurks on every side, so remember that our fight is not against flesh and blood, but against evil, spiritual forces in the heavenly places. We must submit ourselves to the Father and His will, so that we are able to resist the temptations of the evil one. When you remain on guard, when you keep your eyes on Jesus, he will guide you every step of the way.

Pray, Watch, & Wait Devotional

Thursday

Habakkuk 2:1 (NKJV): I will stand my watch; and set myself on the rampart, and watch to see what He will say to me, and what I will answer when I am corrected.

Are we up for the task of standing watch? It involves a combination of listening for the voice of God, and then being obedient when corrected by Him. Habakkuk 1 begins with the prophet crying out to God. He is deeply troubled because of the ungodliness and violence going on around him, especially among God's people. Habakkuk, in his hurt and bitterness, questions if God really cares about their situation. Habakkuk asks God, "Why are you not listening? How long must I cry out to you? Why do I have to watch all of this wickedness and violence?" I'm sure we all have questioned God, I certainly have. We grow impatient, not fully understanding that God's time is not our time. Although we may feel alone, God knows and sees all. An important trait for a believer is longsuffering. It's not easy, but it forces us to put our trust in Him.

Life can be so tough that it's easy for us to forget that God is in charge of all things, and Habakkuk had his moment of doubt as well. When we are going through life's challenges, we want answers and a rescue plan out of our situations. We must remember that God will not put more on us then we can bear. Like Habakkuk, we may become weary in well-doing. As mentioned earlier, we often wander off the path, and go off into a different direction. Despite Habakkuk's moment of doubt, he had a change of heart. In Habakkuk 2, he realized it was time for action; he needed to pray, watch, and wait on God. Habakkuk went before God in a posture of humble submission. We can follow his lead by telling the Lord, "may your will be done, and correct me when I'm wrong." Again, God wants us to be authentic when we pray. He understands and allows us to vent when we pray. However, we cannot forget that God is *omnipresent*; He is present everywhere at the same time. Therefore, we should always be ready to stand at our posts, waiting for the Lord to direct our path.

Pray, Watch, & Wait

Friday

Ephesians 6:18 (NKJV): Praying always with all prayer and supplication in the Spirit, being watchful to this end with all perseverance and supplication for all the saints.

By now, you should know the importance of praying, watching and waiting. In Ephesians, Paul tells us how to properly prepare while waiting on God. In verse 10, he tells us put on the whole armor of God, so you will be ready to stand against all kinds of tricks and schemes of the devil. Remember, we're not fighting actual human beings, but against the evil rulers of wickedness. Satan wants to control us, so he sends armies of demons to attack us from every side. For this reason, we must always be ready, just like a soldier prepares for battle. Gird your waist with truth, which is the Gospel of Jesus Christ. Keep the Word with you, wherever you go. Share it with the lost, and defend it to the end. Put on the breastplate of righteousness, so the enemy cannot penetrate your heart, and the very breath God gave you. The breastplate protects your heart and lungs, which are our most vital organs. Our feet must be secure, so we may carry the gospel of peace. We also need the shield of faith to deflect the fiery darts of the evil one. Never leave home without your helmet of salvation, so that you are protected against the enemy's lies he attempts to put in our heads. Carry your sword, which is the Word of God. Now that you are fully dressed, you are ready for battle! Our Commander and Chief, Jesus Christ, has already won the battle on our behalf. We are Soldiers of the Cross, always prepared and ready to go.

Types of Prayer

If you've been reading up to this point, there should be very little room for doubt about the power of prayer. We have learned that prayer is a dialogue with God, and we must remain steadfast when dealing with life's curve balls. We know challenges come to test our faith, but God is with us. Now, I'm challenging you to kick your prayer life up a notch by understanding the various types of prayer. Before we examine the types of prayers, allow me to revisit my earliest introduction to prayer through my grandmother.

Before going to sleep at my grandmother's house, she would recite the Lord's Prayer with me. When we got to "deliver us from evil," my grandmother would abruptly stop, and tell me to talk to God about anything I needed to talk about, then proceeding with "for thine is the kingdom, power and dominion forever, Amen." For a long time, this was the only way I knew to pray. I believe, with all my heart, that God heard my prayers then as He does now. However, as I grew and accepted Jesus Christ as my Savior, God prompted me to have a stronger prayer life, as I suspect you are also looking to do.

Throughout the day, the type of conversations we have are based largely on who we're talking to. For example, a conversation with a child is drastically different than speaking to a spouse or significant other. A conversation with a co-worker is normally rooted in work-related activities, but when speaking to friends or family, our conversations are more personal and engaging. In a nutshell, our relationship to the other party in a conversation dictates the depth of the conversation. We can think about prayer along these same lines. There are specific prayers for specific situations. Let's take a look at how to include these prayers within our daily prayer life.

Prayer of Adoration
Prayer of Confession
Prayer of Consecration
Prayer of Thanksgiving
Prayer of Supplication
Prayer of Intercession
Prayer of Worship in the Spirit or in Tongues

The Prayer of Adoration is defined as "deep love and respect." When we pray, adoration for God should be the first thing we express, because it shows our devotion, love and respect, for Him.

Revelation 5:13 (NKJV)

And every creature which is in heaven and on the earth and under the earth and such as are in the sea, and all that are in them, I heard saying: "Blessing and honor and glory and power *Be* to Him who sits on the throne, And to the Lamb, forever and ever!"

When we accept Christ as our personal Savior, we have the opportunity to show our adoration for the Father, Son and Holy Ghost every day. However, there will be a time when every knee will bow and every tongue will confess that Jesus is Lord. The scripture says that the angels in heaven, the inhabitants of the earth, and every creature under the earth and the sea, will acknowledge the honor, glory and power of Him who sits on the throne forever. We are created to worship Him, and I, for one, will worship the Father on earth, while I still have breath in me. What do I love about our Heavenly Father? He doesn't force anyone to worship Him; He gives us free will. But one day, we won't have an option. When Christ comes back for His Church, those who chose not to believe shall behold Him. Life on earth is just a rehearsal for everlasting life with Him. Therefore, when you pray, show the Father how much you love and adore Him.

The Prayer of Confession, or acknowledgement, deals with three types of prayer:

1. Confession of sin

2. Confession of God's Word

3. Confession of Satan's lies

Scripture tell us that before salvation, all of us were sinners:

Romans 3:23 (NKJV)

For all have sinned and fall short of the glory of God

However, once we confessed our sin and accepted Jesus as our Lord and Savior, we were forgiven.

1 John 1:9 (NKJV)

If we confess our sins, He is faithful and just to forgive us *our* sins and to cleanse us from all unrighteousness.

After salvation, we are no longer slaves to sin…we're free! Jesus took our sin to the cross.

Romans 6:6 (NKJV)

Knowing this, that our old man was crucified with *Him,* that the body of sin might be done away with, that we should no longer be slaves of sin.

As 'new creatures' in Christ, we are dead to sin, born again, and hopefully not doing the things we did before we were saved. This does not mean we will never do anything wrong—we know this is not the case. Once we accepted Jesus as Savior, we were redeemed by His blood because the Father sees us through the blood of His Son. So, when we make missteps, or sin, we must go before God and confess—with a humble spirit and a repentant heart.

Next, we must confess God's Word, which goes back to what we learned about praying the scriptures. Confess the Word of God on a daily basis because after all, life and death is in the power of the tongue; God's

Word is life, and the enemy's words are death. The key is, whose report will you believe? Satan always comes prepared with false accusations and lies, all disguised to steer us away from God. However, God tells us to stand firm on His Word, for it is true. What will we confess? We are no longer enslaved to sin but free from it through the blood of Jesus Christ. We now live in covenant relationship with the Father, Son, and the Holy Spirit, but we must continually repent. Just as our Father is faithful to forgive us, we must also forgive those who do wrong by us. We have been declared righteous by God, through the blood of Jesus. Just remember, we must confess our sin to God on a daily basis; we must confess the Word of God to remind us of His power, and we must confess or acknowledge the lies of Satan.

The Prayer of Consecration is first seen in the Old Testament, where priests and people presented a sacrifice or offering up to God, as a public display of reverence. This custom meant the sacrifice was for God's use and sanctification. The next scripture speaks about consecration from the New Testament:

Romans 12:1 (NKJV)

I beseech you therefore, brethren, by the mercies of God, that you present your bodies a living sacrifice, holy, acceptable to God, *which is* your reasonable service.

Before Salvation, we lived our lives for personal satisfaction. Since salvation, we present ourselves as living sacrifices unto the Father. In making ourselves available for His use, we are set apart to carry out the works of God. The prayer of consecration is when praying over things or people set aside for God's use.

The Prayer of Thanksgiving is a very simple prayer which expresses gratitude or gives thanks:

Psalm 100:4 (KJV)

Enter into his gates with thanksgiving, *and* into his courts with praise: be thankful unto him, *and* bless his name.

Whenever we enter into the presence of the Lord, we should do so with thanksgiving in our hearts. When should it be prayed? Always.

1 Thessalonians 5:18 (KJV)

In everything give thanks: for this is the will of God in Christ Jesus concerning you.

Regardless of the situation, give thanks. This doesn't mean you are thankful for bad situations, but even while going through tough times, you can still thank God, for He is with you. Pray with a heart of thanksgiving at all times.

The Prayer of Supplication:

Philippians 4:6 (KJV)

Be careful for nothing; but in everything by prayer and supplication with thanksgiving let your requests be made known unto God.

Supplication comes from the Latin verb *supplicare*, which means "to plead humbly." When we ask God for help, we should do so with a humble spirit. Prayers should reflect reverence and devotion, with the confidence in knowing that He alone answers prayer. The Prayer of Supplication is essential when we need the Father to do something in our lives, or the lives of others.

The Prayer of Intercession is the act of intervening on behalf of others. The intercessor knows the battle is not against flesh and blood, (humans) but is warfare against forces and authorities, rulers of darkness, and spiritual powers that can only be won by the King of kings and Lord of lords. The Intercessor is a persistent prayer, always believing that God's will shall prevail. The Holy Spirit invokes intercessors to pray for not only their immediate circle, but for communities, nations and the world:

2 Chronicles 7:14 (KJV)

If my people, which are called by my name, shall humble themselves, and pray, and seek my face, and turn from their wicked ways; then will I hear from heaven, and will forgive their sin, and will heal their land.

The intercessor also knows that God will hear them when they humble themselves before the Father, when they seek His face, when they turn from their wicked ways. The prayers of the righteous avail much. Who are the righteous? Those who have accepted Jesus Christ as Savior. Consequently, we are called to intercede for those whom the Holy Spirit lays on our hearts. As intercessors, we know the battle is not ours but God's. Our battles are fought relying on God's power to destroy fortresses. Intercessory prayer is less about personal needs, but the overall needs of others.

The Prayer of Worship/Spirit/Tongues I coupled these characteristics together because they go together. Not everyone prays in tongues, and in fact, some don't believe in speaking in tongues. Nevertheless, in some of Paul's letters, he talks about speaking and praying in the spirit. I need to write another book on this subject because there is so much more I could say about it. So, I will attempt to explain it in a way that you'll hopefully understand.

Worship is defined as "expressing reverence and adoration to a deity," which is often seen in a church setting. But worship should happen beyond the church walls; we should worship God in everything we do, by giving our best to Him and always putting Him first. Of course, true worship cannot take place until we receive Jesus Christ as our Savior. This is why Jesus said this:

John 4:23-24 (NKJV)

But the hour is coming, and now is, when the true worshipers will worship the Father in spirit and truth; for the Father is seeking such to worship Him. God *is* Spirit, and those who worship Him must worship in spirit and truth."

The Bible describes the Samaritans' worship as defective because they did not have the prophetical writings. The worship of the Jews was described as carnal, in that it was attached to rules and regulations. However, the Gospel of Jesus Christ, displayed the true meaning of all the carnal ordinances and the legal sacrifices in offering Himself, as a living sacrifice. God is a Spirit, and our worship must spring from our heart, which is influenced by the Holy Spirit within us. The Holy Spirit takes over and helps us pray, even when we don't know what to say.

Romans 8:26 (NKJV)

Likewise the Spirit also helps in our weaknesses. For we do not know what we should pray for as we ought, but the Spirit Himself makes intercession for us with groanings which cannot be uttered.

Thank goodness the Holy Spirit interprets our groanings. How often have you tried to get a prayer through, but have been overcome with emotion, doubt, or confusion, that you didn't know what to say? The Father knows our hearts and is able to understand what we are praying for. If you are gifted to speak in tongues, thanks be to God, for you are able to pray and interpret in that heavenly language that only God can understand. Listen to what Paul says:

1 Corinthians 14:5 (NKJV)

I wish you all spoke with tongues, but even more that you prophesied; for he who prophesies *is* greater than he who speaks with tongues, unless indeed he interprets, that the church may receive edification.

1 Corinthians 14:15 (ESV)

¹What am I to do? I will pray with my spirit, but I will pray with my mind also; I will sing praise with my spirit, but I will sing with my mind also.

In these scriptures, Paul tells the Corinthians that it is great to speak in tongues, but even better when the language is interpreted and edifies God. Simply put, if someone speaks in tongues and no one understands what is being said, how does that help the body of Christ? Greater is the one who gives prophesies because if the church understands it, then it edifies the body. Paul is not suggesting that speaking in tongues is irrelevant. What he means is there is a time to pray in the spirit and a time to pray for understanding. If we solely prayed in tongues, who would it benefit? When we are alone in our 'prayer closet,' we can pray in tongues all day long. Public, or corporate prayer, is focused on reaching the masses. If I pray publicly, I don't pray in tongues, or my native language, because those around me would not understand me. When I gather with my prayer partners, we begin by praying for understanding and end with speaking in tongues. I have seen God use members of the group to interpret someone speaking in tongues, followed by providing a word from the Lord. On the other hand, there are times we do not receive an interpretation. One thing is for sure, the Holy Spirit knows all things and searches all things. He will not have anyone confused. In praying the prayer of worship/Spirit/tongues, let's be reminded to worship our Father in spirit and truth. Allow the Holy Spirit to guide you in prayer, for He is the Spirit of Truth. Think of the Holy Spirit as our translator, who transforms our utterances into meaningful prayer. God knows what we are praying for. If you have the gift of speaking in tongues, rest assured that the Holy Spirit will directly tell you when to use your gift. He is not the author of confusion, nor does He want the Body of Christ to be confused.

Take a look at this acronym for *ACTS* which is often used to remember the four types of prayer:

A – Adoration
C – Confession
T – Thanksgiving
S – Supplication

Friends, whenever you pray, use this formula; you cannot go wrong.

TYPES OF PRAYER

Study Questions & Devotionals

1. There are different types of conversations list at least three of them:

   - _____

   - _____

   - _____

2. List three types of prayers:

   - _____

   - _____

   - _____

3. What is the definition for adoration?

   _____

   _____

4. Why should adoration for God be on the forefront of our prayer?

   _____

   _____

5. According to Revelation 5:13 who will worship God?

   _____

   _____

   _____

   _____

6. There are three types of confessions what are they?

   - _____
   - _____
   - _____

7. According to Romans 3:23, who has sinned?

   _____

   _____

8. What cleansing takes place after confession?

   _____

   _____

9. How does God see us after Salvation?

   _____

   _____

10. Give a summary of what confession means?

    _____

    _____

11. What does consecration mean?

    _____

    _____

12. When we present ourselves to God, what do we become? See Romans 12:1

_____

_____

13. Why are we set apart?

_____

_____

14. When should we be thankful?

_____

_____

15. Does giving thanks in everything mean we are giving thanks for bad situations?

_____

_____

16. What does give thanks in everything mean?

_____

_____

_____

_____

17. What does supplication mean?

_____

_____

18. What is the primary function of an intercessor?

_____

_____

19. Who fights the battle?

_____

_____

20. What is our part where the battle is concerned?

_____

_____

21. Define worship.

_____

_____

_____

_____

22. Why was the worship of the Samaritans and Jews defective?

_____

_____

_____

_____

23. What is the only way God can be worshiped?

_____

_____

24. When the Holy Spirit makes intercession, who understands what the Spirit is saying?

_____

_____

25. What are the four types of Prayer?

_____

_____

Types of Prayer Devotional

Monday

We just learned about the various types of prayer. This week, let's begin by applying one or more of the prayers types into our daily devotion. Prayers of adoration expresses our love and devotion when speaking to Him. He is *omnipresent* (everywhere), *omniscient* (all-knowing), and *omnipotent* (unlimited power). He is sovereign, and He is eternal; He is a Spirit and He is alive. In other words, He is everything! When we pray in adoration, we can name some of His attributes. Here is an example:

"Heavenly Father, you are the Lord of all, there is none like you. You are the only true and living God. You are omnipresent, so you are always with me. How I love and adore you. You hold all power in your hand, because you are omnipotent. There is nothing that can get past you, for you know all and hear all- you are omniscient. There is no timetable with you because you are eternal, immortal and invisible, the only true and living God. You are my Father, oh how I love you."

Now write your own prayer of adoration:

_____

_____

_____

_____

_____

_____

_____

Amen.

Types of Prayer Devotional

Tuesday

Today is about the prayer of confession. Although we are saved, we still mess up and need forgiveness. But God is faithful. Confession cleanses us by keeping us in right standing with our Father.

1 John 1:9 (NKJV)

If we confess our sins, He is faithful and just to forgive us *our* sins and to cleanse us from all unrighteousness.

God called David "a man after His own heart." Why did God say this? I believe it's because David freely confessed his sins before God. Remember when Nathan the Prophet confronted David about his sin with Bathsheba? It was after that confrontation that David wrote Psalm 51. David said that his sin was committed against God; he understood the depth of his actions because confession requires humility. Christ died so that we could be forgiven. David prayed "create in me a clean heart Oh God, and renew a right spirit within me." His sin weighed him down. What we need to remember is, once we are saved, we are declared righteous by God. We are no longer sinners, but have been saved by grace.

Like David, we will make mistakes and do wrong. We may even feel the heaviness of our mistake, which should encourage us to humble ourselves and ask for forgiveness on a daily basis. The enemy taunts us by saying, "you are a sinner," and that is a lie. The enemy loves to remind us about our past, before Christ. His guilt trip won't work because once we accepted Jesus into our heart, we were made clean, washed by the blood, and our sinful nature was nailed to the cross. Thanks be to God for His wonderful grace and mercy. The greatest aspect of salvation is that our sins are literally wiped clean. We are free from sin, past, present and future. Moving forward, confess your mistakes and the Word of God. Speak life and not death. Pray, because the Father is waiting to hear from you.

Types of Prayer Devotional

Wednesday

Today is a prayer of consecration, thankfulness, and supplication.

Romans 12:1 (NKJV)

I beseech you therefore, brethren, by the mercies of God, that you present your bodies a living sacrifice, holy, acceptable to God, *which is* your reasonable service.

Friends, have you presented your bodies a living sacrifice, holy, acceptable to God? Every day before you pray, consecrate yourselves by presenting your bodies to the Father. It's simply letting the Father know you are available to be used by Him. I am here, Lord. I belong to you. Use me for your glory today. Then give thanks, as you enter into His gates. Always go before the Father with a thankful heart.

Psalm 100:4 (KJV)

Enter into his gates with thanksgiving, *and* into his courts with praise: be thankful unto him, *and* bless his name.

We have so much to be thankful for, from opening our eyes in the morning to being thankful for our family, home, job, etc. This prayer could go on forever, as we acknowledge the Giver of all things. After giving thanks to God, make your requests known and He will answer you.

Philippians 4:6 (KJV)

Be careful for nothing; but in everything by prayer and supplication with thanksgiving let your requests be made known unto God.

We serve an awesome God who is faithful, just, full of grace, and mercy. Why would we not pray? Prayer is conversing with the one you Love. And how could we not love Him with our whole heart? He loves us so much, He gave us His very best through His Son, Jesus Christ. Therefore, consecrate yourselves, be thankful in all things, make your requests known to the one that knows us better than ourselves, and watch Him use you in the lives of those that don't know Jesus. Here I am Lord, use me, I'll go.

Types of Prayer Devotional

Thursday

Do you ever pray for others? I'm sure you do. We all pray for someone other than ourselves. Intercessory prayer is the act of praying to the Father on behalf of others. There are many examples of intercessory prayer in the Bible. Abraham prayed for Sodom (Gen.18:20-33); Moses interceded for Israel (Exodus 32:11-13); Paul interceded for the Ephesians (Ephesians 3:14-20), the Philippians (Philippians 1:9-11), and the Colossians (Colossians 1:9-12). While the above people were great intercessors, nothing compares to the greatest intercessor ever, Jesus Christ. He made intercession for those formerly in the world, who later became followers of Jesus, just like you and I (John 17:6-26). Jesus used ordinary people, who gave of themselves to be used by God. Prayer changes individual people, nations, and the world. With the Holy Spirit leading and guiding us, we will know who to pray for. Allow Him to guide you in prayer right now.

_____

_____

_____

_____

_____

_____

_____

_____

Types of Prayer Devotional

Friday

What a wonderful privilege to be able to worship the Father, the one who gave us life. Take some time to think about what the Father gave to us, so that we could come boldly before His throne. Jesus suffered, bled and died so that we could begin a new life with a clean slate. If you ever feel down or depressed, know that you were created for good works. You are a member of a royal priesthood; you are the righteousness of God, seated in heavenly places as sons and daughters of the King. Our bodies are the temples of the Holy Spirit, all the more reason to worship the Father in spirit and in truth.

"Oh God, how excellent is your Name in all the earth. Heaven and earth adore you, angels bow before you. You are Lord of Lords and King of Kings, and I worship you. The only true and living God; If I had ten thousand tongues, it would not be enough. But Father, my worship is real. I cry Holy, Holy, Holy, Lord God Almighty. I love and worship you, and until I see you face to face, I will give myself to you, with all my heart. I will worship and proclaim your Name to all I come in contact with, so they too can know the Great and Mighty God I serve."

Now it's your turn to express your worship to the Father:

_____

_____

_____

_____

_____

_____

_____

Halleluiah to the King of Kings!

Trust and Obey

We have come to the last session of the book. If you are anything like me, I love to learn about improving my spiritual walk with God. I trust you have developed a deeper prayer life, filled with more intimacy and meaning than ever before. Perhaps you already knew or heard about some of the topics discussed. However, there are times when we know better, but fail to do better. For example, we know that too much sugar is bad for us, but does that stop us from craving sweet treats? Not at all. It's the same with God's Word. We usually know what the Bible says about certain things, but we just don't always obey. There is an old hymn called "Trust and Obey." I love this hymn, especially this verse: "Trust and obey, for there's no other way to be happy in Jesus, but to trust and obey."

My dear friends, Jesus had to trust and obey His Father. I want you to imagine the last few hours Jesus spent in the Garden of Gethsemane, knowing that he was headed to the cross, to take on the sins of the entire world.

Matthew 26:37-39 (NKJV)

And He took with Him Peter and the two sons of Zebedee, and He began to be sorrowful and deeply distressed. Then He said to them, "My soul is exceedingly sorrowful, even to death. Stay here and watch with Me." He went a little farther and fell on His face, and prayed, saying, "O My Father, if it is possible, let this cup pass from Me; nevertheless, not as I will, but as You *will*."

When I look at this passage, it helps me understand our Savior's humanity and divinity. He fell on His face to pray, a posture requiring deep humiliation. The petitioner would put their head between their knees, with their forehead touching the ground—not a very comfortable position to be in. However, this displayed Jesus' humanity. Jesus then said, "If at all possible, let this cup pass from me, nevertheless not my will, but as you will." In some Biblical references, the cup symbolizes despair, agony, suffering and death. In those times, it was commonplace to force criminals to drink poison. Jesus, an innocent man, drank that bitter cup for you and me. When Jesus said "let this cup pass," it skipped over us and stopped at the cross where He hung to die. This cup represented the sins of the world, so we would not suffer.

Another hymn we often sing is "Pass Me Not, O Gentle Savior." One of the verses says: "Pass me not, o gentle Savior; Hear my humble cry; While on others thou art calling, do not pass me by." Rather than allowing the cup to pass from Him, Jesus obeyed His Father's will, which created the greatest gift of all, Eternal Life.

Anyone who calls on the name of Jesus, by acknowledging that He is the Son of God, and confessing one's sins, shall be saved. It's that simple, no additional steps or processes. God made it so simple for man to come to Him.

Romans 10:9 (NKJV)

That if you confess with your mouth the Lord Jesus and believe in your heart that God has raised Him from the dead, you will be saved.

Pretty simple, right? Unfortunately, man likes to add conditions or terms of salvation. There are no stipulations other than what the scriptures says: confess with your mouth, and believe in your heart that God raised Him from the dead. We cannot add or take away anything from that. We have a tendency to view saved people as perfect. I'm so sorry to disappoint you, but once we're saved, there's a process called sanctification. Sanctification is the work of God's free grace, whereby everyone who has accepted Jesus into their heart is renewed in the whole man after the image of God; it enables us to die to sin, and to live in righteousness. Sanctification sets us apart so God may use us. The more we grow in our spiritual walk, the more Christ-like we become on a daily basis. So, when we witness saved people doing wrong, don't forget that we all miss the mark at times.

We are all under construction, which is why we cannot rely on our own strength. God molds us to become more like Christ. Our job is to continuously demonstrate our faith in Christ by obeying His commands. The Holy Spirit is the key to this process. If we walk in the power of the Holy Spirit, we will not give in to our fleshly desires to gratify lust. God has already provided us the tools to help us along this sanctification process.

1) Follow the map, which is the Bible, also known as, the "**B**asic **I**nstructions **B**efore **L**eaving **E**arth". Through reading and studying the Word of God, we will have understanding.

2) Prayer is the direct line of communication to God that allows us to go before Him at any time. He wants to hear from us.

3) Fellowship with other believers because it helps us to grow. Iron sharpens iron.

4) Read biblically-based teachings, like this book, to strengthen your daily walk.

5) Share the gospel with those that are lost. Let it bring a source of joy in knowing you were responsible for building the kingdom of God.

Folks, trust God, and obey His will for our lives. When we do this, God is faithful to take us to places we never imagined. He will use us for His glory, especially in the lives of those we come in contact with. Obedience is always better than sacrifice. God's love and power is infinite—it has no end. I must confess…in writing this book, I have gone deeper in my payer life as well, so much so that God wanted me to write about it. I'm so grateful that my Father used me; He trusted me with this work. May this book serve as an additional resource as you study the Word of God. May it bless you, and those you share it with. My prayer is that *Going into the Deep Through Prayer* forever changes your life, as it has mine. May your walk with the Father, Son and Holy Spirit continue here to eternity.

Friends, nothing or no one can ever separate you from the love of God. I am humbled and grateful to share my experiences and the Word of God with you. Be blessed!

Numbers 6:24-26 (NKJV) "The LORD bless you and keep you; The LORD make His face shine upon you, and be gracious to you; The LORD lift up His countenance upon you, and give you peace." Amen.

TRUST & OBEY

Study Questions & Devotionals

Matthew 26:37-39 (NKJV)

And He took with Him Peter and the two sons of Zebedee, and He began to be sorrowful and deeply distressed. Then He said to them, "My soul is exceedingly sorrowful, even to death. Stay here and watch with Me." He went a little farther and fell on His face, and prayed, saying, "O My Father, if it is possible, let this cup pass from Me; nevertheless, not as I will, but as You *will.*"

1. Looking at this passage, how can you tell the difference between Jesus' humanity and his divinity?

_____

_____

_____

_____

2. Jesus fell on His face praying, why was this a posture of pain?

_____

_____

_____

_____

3. In sacred writings the cup was often used to point out what?

_____

_____

_____

_____

4. The cup which contained poison, was used for criminals, when Jesus took the cup what was He doing and who did He do it for?

_____

_____

_____

_____

Romans 10:9 (NKJV)

That if you confess with your mouth the Lord Jesus and believe in your heart that God has raised Him from the dead, you will be saved.

5. According to this scripture, what is required to be saved?

_____

_____

_____

_____

6. After Salvation there is a process we go through, what is it called?

_____

_____

7. What are some tools that can help us grow?

_____

_____

_____

_____

NOTES:

Trust & Obey Devotional

Monday

There are many promises in the Word of God, but one of my favorite scriptures comes from Proverbs 3:5-6. Every day, I am reminded of this powerful message, because in every situation, I need to trust God:

Proverbs 3:5-6 (NKJV)

Trust in the LORD with all your heart, and lean not on your own understanding; In all your ways acknowledge Him, And He shall direct your paths.

What stands out to me in this particular text is removing the burden of trusting in self, my parents, family or friends, but in the LORD. More importantly, I must trust Him with my whole heart, not halfheartedly. Trusting Him is only part of our responsibility; we must also obey Him by not leaning to our own understanding. I have often followed my own understanding and disobeyed the will of God, which led to the wrong path. Now I pray, "Father, I trust you with my whole heart. Order my steps and direct my path. If you give me direction, I can walk in the right path." What areas of your life have you failed to truly entrust to the Father?

Take a couple of moments to recall the times you've leaned on your own understanding. After our trip down memory lane, we now have to acknowledge God's sovereignty, so He may direct our path. God wants to lead us in everything we do. He does not want to ride in the back seat; God wants to be the driver of our lives. He is standing by, waiting for us to acknowledge Him during our daily routines. Believe it or not, I even ask the Father to help me choose an outfit for the day, or to help me with my hair! Guess what? He is right there to direct me. Start leaning on God for everything. He wants to be involved in every aspect of our lives.

Trust & Obey Devotional

Tuesday

One of my favorite songs is "Order My Steps" by the GMWA Women of Worship. The lyrics are powerful:

Order my steps in Your word dear Lord
Lead me, guide me every day
Send Your anointing, Father I pray;
Order my steps in Your word
Please, order my steps in Your word

Humbly, I ask Thee teach me Your will
While You are working, help me be still
'Cause Satan is busy, God is real;
Order my steps in Your word
Please, order my steps in Your word

Bridle my tongue let my words edify
Let the words of my mouth be acceptable in Thy sight
Take charge of my thoughts both day and night;
Order my steps in Your word
Please order my steps in Your word

I want to walk worthy
According to Thy will
Please order my steps Lord
And I'll do Your blessed will
The world is ever changing
But You are still the same;
Please order my steps, Lord I'll praise Your name

Order my steps in Your word
Order my tongue in Your word
Guide my feet in Your word

Wash my heart in Your word
Show me how to walk in Your word
Show me how to talk in Your word
When I need a brand-new song to sing
Show me how to let Your praises ring
In your word

Please order my steps in Your word

Why don't you make this your prayer for today? Then trust and obey.

Trust & Obey Devotional

Wednesday

Jesus had to trust and obey His Father all the way to Calvary. Because of His obedience, God made it possible for us to have access to Jesus, through the shedding of His blood. I'm so thankful Jesus was obedient, unlike our inconsistent nature. However, we have prime examples of people who put their trust in God. Look at Abraham. He obeyed God, and left the comforts of home to follow God's calling on his life. Despite all of the obstacles Joseph faced, his trust and obedience in God allowed him to walk into destiny. Hey, if you've been reading this book and studying the Word, you have also been committed and obedient.

The more time we spend in God's Word, the more we will get out of it. This principle is true in every aspect of life. From exercising for better health to planting a garden that yields food, doing the upfront work eventually produces results. 2 Timothy 2:15 says "to study so that we can show ourselves approved to God, a workman that does not need to be ashamed, rightly dividing the word of truth." When we talk to others about our Father, we don't want to give our opinion, because that doesn't matter. We should be able to explain the Word to them so that they can better understand it. If God determines we are the vessel to lead someone to Christ, we must be ready. The way to do this is by studying and knowing God's Word, and by living it out so others can see Jesus in you. Trust and obey His Word.

Trust & Obey Devotional

Thursday

"There will be no peace in any soul until it is willing to obey the voice of God."
D.L. Moody

Obedience is yielding to the will of God. As mentioned earlier, God never forces us to do anything. Accepting Jesus as our Savior was a personal decision. Although we are now saved, God still does not force us to follow his path…it's still our decision. But if we are believers, then we will obey Him and keep His Word.

John 14:23 (NKJV)

Jesus answered and said to him, "If anyone loves Me, he will keep My word; and My Father will love him, and We will come to him and make Our home with him.

Trusting and obeying God produces fellowship with the Trinity: God the Father, who is the head of our lives; Jesus as our Savior; the Holy Spirit who leads and guides us from within. We have to make a conscious decision to serve, trust and obey the Lord. I'm like Joshua, "as for me and my house, we will serve the Lord." How about you? Have you decided to trust and obey today?

Trust & Obey Devotional

Friday

Acts 5:29 (NKJV)

But Peter and the *other* apostles answered and said: "We ought to obey God rather than men.

We must obey God rather than men. Does that mean that we disregard authority and do what we want? Of course not. Obeying God creates alignment; everything else has no choice but to fall into place. In other words, God would not guide you into doing something illegal. In fact, following God encourages us to challenge those that are doing wrong. When we follow and trust God, our conscience does not want to grieve the Holy Spirit, especially things that are contrary to the will of God.

Friends, as you complete the last devotional of this prayer guide, let me share a couple of quotes to encourage you as you go deeper in prayer:

"Never be afraid to trust an unknown future to a known God." - **Corrie Ten Boom**

"Trusting God does not mean believing he will do what you want, but rather believing he will do everything he knows is good." - **Ken Sande**

"Pray and let God worry." - **Martin Luther**

"When God takes out the trash, don't go digging back through it. Trust Him." - **Amaka Imani Nkosazana**

"You say to God, I have never seen you provide for me." God says to you, *"You have never trusted Me."* - **Corallie Buchanan**

"Trusting and obeying God yields peace, prosperity and life everlasting." **Anna Hawthorne**

Printed in the United States
by Baker & Taylor Publisher Services